W9-ATY-410

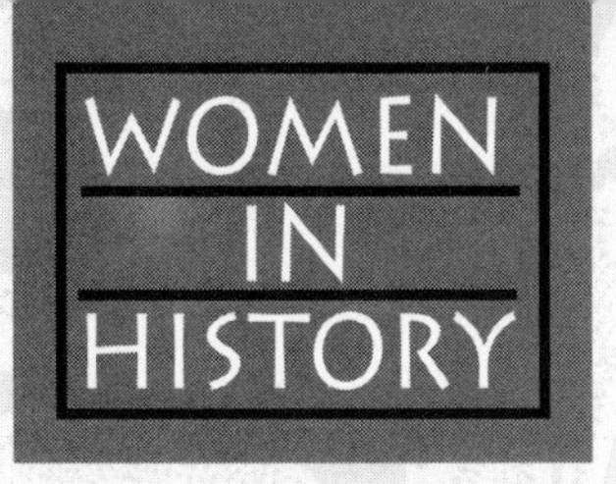

Women of the American Frontier

Stuart A. Kallen

San Diego • Detroit • New York • San Francisco • Cleveland • New Haven, Conn. • Waterville, Maine • London • Munich

For more information, contact
Lucent Books
27500 Drake Rd.
Farmington Hills, MI 48331-3535
Or you can visit our Internet site at http://www.gale.com

LIBRARY OF CONGRESS CATALOGING-IN-PUBLICATION DATA

Kallen, Stuart A., 1955–
Women of the American frontier / by Stuart A. Kallen.
p. cm. — (Women in history)
Includes bibliographical references and index.
ISBN 1-59018-471-8 (hard cover : alk. paper)
1. Women pioneers—United States—History—Juvenile literature. 2. Women pioneers—West (U.S.)—History—Juvenile literature. 3. Frontier and pioneer life—United States—Juvenile literature. 4. Frontier and pioneer life—West (U.S.)—Juvenile literature. 5. United States—Social life and customs—Juvenile literature. 6. West (U.S.)—Social life and customs—Juvenile literature. I. Title. II. Series: Women in history (San Diego, Calif.)
E179.5.K353 2004
978'.02'082—dc22

2004010203

Printed in the United States of America

Contents

Foreword

The story of the past as told in traditional historical writings all too often leaves the impression that if men are not the only actors in the narrative, they are assuredly the main characters. With a few notable exceptions, males were the political, military, and economic leaders in virtually every culture throughout recorded time. Since traditional historical scholarship focuses on the public arenas of government, foreign relations, and commerce, the actions and ideas of men—or at least of powerful men—are naturally at the center of conventional accounts of the past.

In the last several decades, however, many historians have abandoned their predecessors' emphasis on "great men" to explore the past "from the bottom up," a phenomenon that has had important consequences for the study of women's history. These social historians, as they are known, focus on the day-to-day experiences of the "silent majority"—those people typically omitted from conventional scholarship because they held relatively little political or economic sway within their societies. In the new social history, members of ethnic and racial minorities, factory workers, peasants, slaves, children, and women are no longer relegated to the background but are placed at the very heart of the narrative.

Around the same time social historians began broadening their research to include women and other previously neglected elements of society, the feminist movement of the late 1960s and 1970s was also bringing unprecedented attention to the female heritage. Feminists hoped that by examining women's past experiences, contemporary women could better understand why and how gender-based expectations had developed in their societies, as well as how they might reshape inherited—and typically restrictive—economic, social, and political roles in the future.

Today, some four decades after the feminist and social history movements gave new impetus to the study of women's history, there is a rich and continually growing body of work on all aspects of women's lives in the past. The Lucent Books Women in History series draws upon this abundant and diverse literature to introduce students to women's experiences within a variety of past cultures and time periods in terms of the distinct roles they filled. In their capacities as workers, activists, and artists, women exerpted significant influence on important events whether they conformed to or broke from traditional roles. The Women in History titles depict extraordinary women who managed to attain positions of influence in their male-dominated societies, including such celebrated heroines as the feisty medieval queen Eleanor of Aquitaine, the brilliant propagandist of the American Revolution Mercy Otis Warren, and the courageous African American activist of the Civil War era Harriet Tubman. Included as well are the stories of the ordinary—and often overlooked—women of the past who also helped shape their societies myriad ways—moral, intellectual, and economic—without straying far from customary gender roles: the housewives and mothers, school teachers and church volunteers, midwives and nurses and wartime camp followers.

In this series, readers will discover that many of these unsung women took more significant parts in the great political and social upheavals of their day than has often been recognized. In *Women of the American Revolution,* for example, students will learn how American housewives assumed a crucial role in helping the Patriots win the war against Britain. They accomplished this by planting and harvesting fields, producing and trading goods, and doing whatever else was necessary to maintain the family farm or business in the absence of their soldier husbands despite the heavy burden of housekeeping and child-care duties they already bore. By their self-sacrificing actions, competence, and ingenuity, these anonymous heroines not only kept their families alive, but kept the economy of their struggling young nation going as well during eight long years of war.

Each volume in this series contains generous commentary from the works of respected contemporary scholars, but the Women in History series particularly emphasizes quotations from primary sources such as diaries, letters, and journals whenever possible to allow the women of the past to speak for themselves. These firsthand accounts not only help students to better understand the dimensions of women's daily spheres—the work they did, the organizations they belonged to, the physical hardships they faced—but also how they viewed themselves and their actions in the light of their society's expectations for their sex.

The distinguished American historian Mary Beard once wrote that women have always been a "force in history." It is hoped that the books in this series will help students to better appreciate the vital yet often little-known ways in which women of the past have shaped their societies and cultures.

Introduction: The American Frontier

From the first years that Europeans settled in North America in the 1600s, the frontier shifted constantly. As the population grew along the East Coast, there were thousands of women and men who felt the call to push beyond the relative tameness of villages and towns and into the wilderness. In the West, vast forests, mountains, rivers, and lakes of the American continent remained in their natural state.

By the 1750s the East Coast was filling with new immigrants, and Americans began streaming into the dense Appalachian woodlands of present-day Kentucky, Tennessee, West Virginia, and the western Carolinas. As this area was settled and "tamed," the border of the frontier crept ever westward, with pioneers pushing across the Mississippi River by 1840. In the following decades, the American frontier shifted to the far west of North America. Thousands of emigrants crossed the western prairies, mountains, and deserts. These emigrants did not settle the continent's interior. Instead, they continued until they reached California, Oregon, and Washington. Then, as the best lands were taken along the coastal region, the tide of immigration swept back to the east and south, with immigrants settling the frontier regions in the Rocky Mountains and on the plains in the Midwest, from Texas to Kansas to Minnesota.

Wherever the line marking the frontier was located, within ten to twenty years after the arrival of the first pioneers, the terrain had changed from wilderness to settled lands dotted with communities that resembled those in the East. The numbers tell the story of this great migration to the frontier. In 1840 only 1 percent of all Americans lived west of the Mississippi River. By 1890, however, more than 350,000 had moved to new farms and towns west of the river—a number equal to about 20 percent of the U.S. population at the time.

Searching for Wealth and Health

As this ever-moving frontier suggests, nineteenth-century Americans were a restless people. They were spurred west by books, magazines, and newspapers that described the frontier as a paradise, a place where people could be free while growing wealthy. The reality of frontier life, however, was often quite the opposite. The land characterized by whites as empty frontier already belonged to hundreds of thousands of Native Americans, who frequently clashed with the white settlers who took their ancestral lands. In addition, clearing land for farms, scratching a living from the soil, and surviving in an often hostile natural environment was dangerous, backbreaking work. This was especially true for women of the American frontier. Men were often absent for long periods—off hunting, searching for gold, or fighting Indians. Sometimes, a man never returned. Women were left to fend for themselves, all the while caring for children, making or mending clothes, cooking, looking after the farm, and tending to dozens of other physically demanding chores.

Woman's Rights in the Nineteenth Century

Frontier women operated at a disadvantage in a culture that treated females differently from men. It was a time of high

A woman chops firewood as her family makes camp along the frontier. As the East Coast became settled, large numbers of Americans began to migrate west in search of land.

concern for morals, modesty, and proper decorum. Women were viewed as delicate, asexual creatures who were given few rights. Society deemed that a wife "belonged" to her husband. He had all rights to her property, while she had none to his. A woman who committed adultery could go to jail for up to three months in some places; men committing the same act were rarely punished.

Another aspect of gender inequality was women's lack of voice in issues of childbearing. Birth control was practically nonexistent, and abortions were uncommon. As a result, most nineteenth-century women spent most of their adult lives either pregnant or nursing babies.

Legally, women were strictly dependent on men. The U.S. Constitution did not mention the rights of women, and females could not vote in most places. A woman could not own property, make a will, enter a contract, or sue in court without her husband's consent. Only men had the legal right to custody of children. Courts rarely granted a divorce upon a woman's request unless the husband had deserted her or was a serious alcoholic.

Such unequal treatment was accepted because it was believed that a woman's only mission in life was to serve a man. The nation's clergymen promoted that idea. In 1808 the Reverend Samuel Miller wrote:

> How interesting and important are the duties devolved on females as WIVES . . . the counsellor and friend of the husband; who makes it her daily study to lighten his cares, to soothe his sorrows, and augment his joys; who, like a guardian angel, watches over his interests, warns him against dangers, comforts him under trials; and by her pious, assiduous, and attractive deportment, constantly endeavors to render him more virtuous, more useful, more honorable, and more happy.[1]

Women on the Frontier

The Reverend Samuel Miller's words make it clear that nineteenth-century society looked upon women as caretakers of civilization and guardians of morals. In the harsh frontier environment, women played important roles in creating homes, communities, churches, schools, and other institutions.

Yet the frontier also provided new opportunities for independence for some women. Throwing off the restrictions of society, some women fought the odds to become business owners, restaurateurs, innkeepers, saloon keepers, cowgirls, peddlers, and more. They wielded firearms to put food on the table and worked in mines. A few even dressed as men and served as trail guides and military scouts, roles that were otherwise closed to women.

The gleaming cities of the modern American West owe their origins to the pioneers who set out for the frontier with little more than dreams. The willing hands and strong spirits of thousands of women helped build the wilderness communities that grew into cities. From the Appalachian Mountains to the Pacific Ocean, women of the American frontier made an indelible mark on the land and shaped the destiny of the United States.

Chapter 1: Women on the Appalachian Frontier

In the middle of the eighteenth century, the vast North American continent to the west was virtually unknown to European settlers who lived along the eastern seaboard. Most of these relatively recent immigrants lived within twenty miles of the Atlantic Ocean. Westward migration was largely blocked by the sixteen-hundred-mile-long system of mountains known as the Appalachians, which presented a seemingly impenetrable barrier to travelers on foot and horseback. This was particularly true from Pennsylvania south through North Carolina and westward into Tennessee. In these areas, broad mountain chains, known today as the Blue Ridge, Smoky, Black, and Cumberland mountains, average three thousand feet above sea level; some peaks rise to heights of more than sixty-six hundred feet.

Would-be settlers, however, sought to overcome this barrier. In the mid–eighteenth century, the eastern slopes of the Appalachians were explored by hunters, trappers, and scouts searching for a pass that would ease the journey west. That pass was finally discovered in 1750 by an Englishman named Thomas Walker, who was an agent for a Virginia land company. This natural gap, located 1,665 feet above sea level, and located in the towering mountains where the borders of Kentucky, Tennessee, and Virginia meet, Walker named the Cumberland Gap. Native Americans had been using this pass for centuries as they hunted the wild animals that migrated through the area. West of the gap, a system of Indian trails branched out to the south and west.

In the years following Walker's discovery, people began moving west, as the eastern seaboard began filling rapidly with European immigrants. After the American Revolution ended in 1783, about 250,000 poor Germans came to the United States to escape wars, persecution, and bad harvests. A quarter million Scottish ran from high rents and poor lands in Scotland and northern England. Half a million others came from elsewhere in Europe. Motivated by stories of a paradise in the wilderness, many of these immigrants eventually traveled through the Cumberland Gap to the wide area simply called Kentucky. Many families left civilization with only an ax, a rifle, an iron pot, a few crude tools, packets of seeds, bedding, and the clothes on their backs.

During the heyday of this migration, between 1775 and 1800, some two hundred thousand to three hundred thousand men, women, and children from all walks of life crossed the Cumberland Gap. They settled in the Appalachians, and the population grew at an amazing rate. By 1800 over seven hundred thousand settlers lived west of the Appalachians, where there were virtually none in 1770.

"A Feminine Touch"

Whereas men had long made brief forays into the Appalachians in order to hunt and trap, families came to stay, and women sought to create a semblance of home life. For example, in September 1775, three families arrived at a small settlement consisting of ten log cabins in a village known as Harrodsburg, southwest of present-day Lexington, Kentucky. The travelers' wives, known only as Mrs. Hugh McGary, Mrs. Thomas Denton, and Mrs. Richard Hogan, were the first white women to settle in Kentucky. In their roles as traditional eighteenth-century homemakers, the women quickly improved the crude log cabins that had been built earlier by the men, as George Morgan Chinn writes in *Kentucky Settlements and Statehood, 1750–1800:*

> The women soon added a feminine touch to Harrodsburg and transformed the rough hunters' cabins into homes suitable for families.

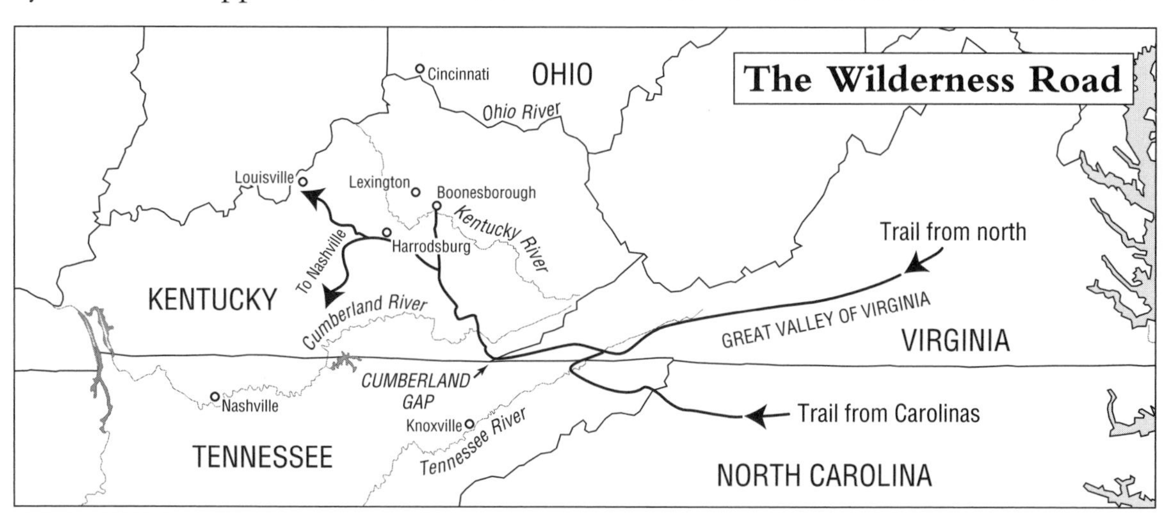

> They selected large flat stones from the creekbed for hearths. Sturdy wooden doors with leather hinges were hung and openings were cut in the log walls and covered with greased deerskin to make windows.[2]

Around the same time, in another part of Kentucky, Daniel Boone brought about thirty settlers, including his wife, Rebecca, and his daughter, Jemima, to the small settlement of Boonesborough. As had happened in Harrodsburg, the women had a civilizing effect on the tiny wilderness community. As George Washington Ranck wrote in 1901 in *Boonesborough*, "Life was transformed as though by magic: shaving, hair-cutting, washing, sweeping, knitting, quilting, and 'courtin' began—even looking glasses [mirrors] came into use. Life was better at Boonesborough."[3]

"Part of the Fighting Force"

While women added a touch of domesticity to life in Boonesborough, they were sometimes called upon to defend the settlement. When more than four hundred Native Americans surrounded the town, men and women retreated to the local fort. According to Ranck, the women "should be listed as part of the fighting force, for in courage and marksmanship they were not to be despised. . . . [The fort's commander Colonel Callaway] told the women to put on hats and hunting shirts and appear as men and get on top of the walls [so] that they might appear as a great many men."[4] The ploy worked. Before long, peaceful gestures were made between the opposing forces, and a feast was held as a token of good faith.

As more settlers flooded into the wilderness, however, Native Americans became increasingly hostile toward the intruders trespassing upon their ancestral lands. When parties of travelers were attacked, women were often forced to assume roles that they could hardly have imagined in the East. Some did so with great bravery. In the 1852 book *The Pioneer Women of the West*, Elizabeth F. Ellet describes a 1780 canoe trip through the Tennessee wilderness, where Cherokee and Chickasaw warriors perched high on surrounding cliffs fired their guns at the pioneers as they floated past:

> When the crew were thrown into disorder and dismay [a young woman, Nancy Gower,] took the helm, and steered the boat, exposed to all the fire of the enemy. A [musket] ball passed through her thigh, going out the opposite side. It was not discovered that she was wounded by any complaint she made, or a word she uttered, but after the danger was over, her mother dis-

Rebecca Boone

Daniel Boone remains one of the most famous explorers of the Appalachian frontier, and his adventures have become the stuff of legend. As Boone carved successive homesteads out of the wilderness, he was aided by his wife, Rebecca. In *The Pioneer Women of the West,* Elizabeth F. Ellet describes Rebecca Boone's roles as adventurer, mother, and homemaker:

> [Daniel Boone] went to explore the unsettled regions of [western] North Carolina. When he had selected a locality near the head waters of the Yadkin [River], Rebecca, with the same resolute spirit of enterprise which afterwards led her to the wilds of Kentucky, bade farewell to her friends, and followed her adventurous husband. In a few months her home had assumed a pleasant aspect; a neat cabin stood on a pleasant eminence near the river, surrounded by an enclosed field; the farm was well stocked, and with the abundance of game in the woods, the settlers had no lack of means for comfort and enjoyment . . . while as yet the surrounding forest was untouched by an axe. For some years the young couple lived in this sylvan [wooded] retirement. . . . [Eventually] Boone made up his mind to remove to some wilder spot [in Kentucky]. . . .
>
> [Mrs. Boone showed she possessed] the same energy, heroism, and firmness which [Daniel] had shown in all the vicissitudes of his eventful career, with the gentler qualities by which woman as the centre of the domestic system, diffuses happiness and trains her children to become useful and honored in the after life. Having shared willingly in the hardships, labors and dangers of those adventurers whose names live in grateful remembrance, she is entitled to some of the portion of the renown that has embalmed them.

covered the blood flowing through her clothes.[5]

Women who could not fight back for whatever reason were sometimes kidnapped and used as slaves. In the late 1780s, Jane Brown was taken into captivity, and according to Ellet, "She found herself a slave, doomed to bear wood and water, pound hominy [corn], and do all the servile offices for her [Indian] mistress."[6] Brown's sorrow was compounded when her nine-year-old son and seven-year-old daughter were taken from her and sent to other villages.

A Home in the Wilderness

Despite the dangers, settler families continued to flood into the Appalachian wilderness. After finding a piece of land safe from attack and with adequate water and timber supplies, men and women worked together to ensure their survival on the frontier. The first order of business was the construction of temporary shelters, which were often crude lean-tos made from poles, brush, and mud. As with most other aspects of frontier life, women played an important role in the assembly of these crude buildings. Men cut saplings for the buildings while women cleared the ground to make space for the floor. Two forked posts were anchored in the ground to support a strong crossbeam. Large logs and saplings were then leaned across the crossbeam, forming a roof. Women took on the task of mixing up

A frontier family prepares dinner in front of their temporary prairie shelter. Once a family found land to settle, the women and men worked together to assemble shelter as quickly as possible.

buckets of mud while men piled brush on top of the timbers. As women and older children carried the heavy mud to the men, it was poured onto the roof in hopes that once it had dried it would protect the occupants from the elements.

As men finished the exterior, women did their best to make the lean-to into a comfortable family shelter. They lined the interior with pelts from bear, wolf, buffalo, and wildcats. Pelts also served as flooring, mattresses, blankets, and pillows.

As the months passed, in their spare time, men would gather materials for a log cabin. Using axes and other hand tools, they cut trees, stripped the bark, and notched logs. When enough material was in place, neighbors would come from miles around for a "cabin raising." Once again, women were assigned mud duties, mixing dirt and water to make the mud to fill in the spaces between the logs.

Cooking in the Rough

Even as women fulfilled their roles as construction workers, they were also obligated to feed their families, and in the roughest circumstance imaginable. Those living in lean-tos gathered flat rocks to make large fire pits on the open sides of the shelter. Fires were kept alive day and night for cooking, to provide warmth, and to discourage wild animals from entering the lean-to.

Cooking in a fire pit was an arduous task. Coals were raked under individual pots to regulate heat. Each fireplace had a long metal pole thrust across it; from this, cast-iron pots were suspended by pot hooks. Large pots—weighing up to forty pounds when full—were used for boiling liquids, rendering fat, simmering soups and stews, and curing meats. When washing was to be done, the pots were used to boil dirty clothes. Pioneer Miriam Colt described her cooking situation in her nineteenth-century diary:

> Have a fire out of doors to cook by; two [notched sticks] driven into the ground, with a round pole laid thereon, on which hang our kettles and camp pails, stones laid up at the ends and back to make it as much as it can be in the form of a fireplace, so as to keep our fire, ashes, and all, from blowing high and dry, when these fierce . . . winds blow. It is not very agreeable work, cooking out of doors in this windy, rainy weather, or when the scorching sun shines.[7]

Frying was done in large, long-handled, three-legged, cast-iron frying pans placed directly over the coals. Maneuvering these heavy vessels filled with boiling liquids and hot foods was a dangerous enterprise. Thousands of women were severely burned or even killed in cooking accidents. The long dresses, petticoats, or aprons women wore often caught on fire. As Colt writes, "The bottoms of our dresses are burnt full of holes now and will soon be burnt off."[8]

In addition to cooking, most women had to make the kitchen implements they used every day. Hickory brooms were made from saplings that were carefully slivered by housewives wielding sharp knives. A bowl could be made by using hot cinders to burn a hollow in a chunk of maple and then scraping it out further with a flat piece of metal. Spoons, forks, and platters were whittled and shaped from poplar, buckeye, or basswood. Dried gourds were fashioned into ladles, dippers, cups, buckets, and bowls. This use for gourds made their seeds among the most important items packed by women before they left civilization to move into the wilderness.

Women also acted as potters in places where good clay was to be found. Housewives shaped plates, bowls, and cups and, after drying the objects, saturated them with bear or other animal grease so they would be waterproof.

Hunting and Fishing

Whatever they did, frontier women had to be self-reliant, since men were often absent. Some men were called away to join military campaigns, others left to further explore the wilderness. Thousands of men died from illness, accidents, or less frequently, the wounds suffered in clashes with Indians. The absence of men was so common, in fact, that historians have coined the term "women in waiting" to describe those on the frontier waiting—often in vain—for their husbands to return.

Women in waiting had to add to their duties those of their spouses. It was often left to them to become hunters—tracking, killing, and dressing game animals such as deer, wild turkeys, ducks, geese, squirrels, and rabbit. This game, along with the plentiful fish that swam in lakes and rivers, was the basis of the frontier family's diet.

In addition to bringing home meat, women were also farmers who harvested a cornucopia of fresh foods for their families. These foods included apples, asparagus, beans, cabbages, pears, peas, potatoes, pumpkins, radishes, raspberries, strawberries, wild grapes, plums, walnuts, chestnuts, and pecans. What was not eaten fresh was preserved as pickles, jams, and jellies in clay jars. Corn was dried and pounded into fine meal with large mortars made from logs. Cornmeal mixed with water, bear grease, or butter was baked into a tasty corn bread known as johnnycake. Herbs, roots, and other wild plants were harvested for teas and medicines. These were sweetened with wild honey and with syrup made from the sap of maple trees.

Women were also in charge of tending the cows, goats, chickens, sheep, and pigs that pioneer families brought with them into the wilderness. Eggs were gathered and milk was churned into butter or made into cheese. If a woman had an abundance of these foods, she could use them to barter with the neighbors for whatever items she lacked.

The Work of Weaving

What frontier women often lacked was the means of keeping their families clothed. Women had to be weavers, seamstresses, dyers, shoemakers, and hatmakers. With a scarcity of traditional materials such as cotton and flax, women often improvised new ways to make cloth. For example, Appalachian women utilized spinning wheels to twist bear and buffalo fur with wild nettles and milkweed into a course yarn that could be woven into cloth on a loom.

Frontier women learned other means of making clothes from the Native Americans. Rabbit, wildcat, and raccoon skins were formed into hats; deer, or buckskin, was ideal for moccasins, leggings, jackets, and other items once it had been tanned. Tanning the hide, however, was labor intensive. To accomplish this, women had to soak the deer hide in lye to soften it, scrape the flesh from the skin, soften the hide by rubbing it for days with a solution made from mashed deer brains boiled in water and grease and, finally, stretch it by hand onto a drying frame and smoke it over oak chips.

In later years, sheep became more abundant on the frontier and women carded, spun, and knitted wool to create all manner of household items. The cloth was often dyed with substances women found in the woods, such as walnut for brown, sumac berries for red, hickory bark for yellow, oak and maple leaves for purple, and peach leaves for green. A single skilled weaver could create an amazing amount of cloth. Writing in 1897, Sarah E. Soper described the wool produced by her mother in the 1830s:

> In the early years of married life, my mother not only helped in the farm work, but took in spinning . . . and in this way her family [was] supplied with all the necessary woolen garments for winter wear, from the woolen socks and stockings, to the dresses, coats and pants, besides all the wool home-made blankets and sheets for the bed. . . . [Her] brother-in-law, being a carpenter, made her a

Holding Back the Tears

Many women who journeyed into the wilderness beyond the Appalachians felt a deep sense of loneliness and isolation in a wild, unknown land. One such woman was Rebecca Ives Gilman, who was forced to move to the Ohio backwoods after her husband's profitable business failed in Exeter, New Hampshire. In *The Land Before Her*, Ann Kolodny describes Gilman's anguish and her need to hold back her tears for her husband:

> [The] forty-two-year-old [Rebecca Ives Gilman] who had been so unceremoniously ushered out of her beloved Exeter home to begin the long trek over the [Appalachian] mountains had not happily or easily adapted to life in the fledgling Marietta settlement at Fort Harmar [in Ohio]. Years later, Rebecca Ives Gilman, now "an old lady bowed by affliction more than by years," confided a description of quite different experience to her old friend from Exeter. As the friend [Mary H. Emery] reported it, "She told me that she had learned to milk the cow and used to sit with the pail and looking up to heaven, say 'Are these the stars and the moon I used to see at Exeter?' And sob and cry as loud as a child, and then wipe her tears and appear before her husband as cheerful as if she had nothing to give her pain." The stars and the moon, of course, were the same. But nothing else on that frontier held their familiarity. Still . . . Rebecca Ives Gilman . . . went meekly westward and held back her tears before those who had brought her, against her will, into the wilderness. . . .

To Rebecca Ives Gilman, the journey with her husband and son from the established and cultured town of Exeter to the edge of the frontier at the wooded confluence of the Ohio and Muskingum rivers, surrounded by hostile Indian tribes, must have seemed like removal to a desolate wilderness, indeed.

loom, and with this, for more than twenty years, she provided many comforts for her family of four daughters and a son; besides, in this way [she] laid up money to help build the new house, never from the beginning falling short of weaving upwards of 1,000 yards, and going as high as 1,800 or 2,000 yards in some few years.[9]

Making Quilts

In addition to clothing, women had to make many other items for their households, including sheets, bedspreads, pillows, towels, tablecloths, and napkins. As with making clothing, women utilized ingenious ways to make their families comfortable. For example, scraps of cloth and rags were sewn end to end and rolled into large balls. When sufficient material was available, it was woven into rag rugs on a loom. Scraps of cloth were also used to make quilts.

Making quilts served several purposes. Beside creating useful bedding items, the process allowed women to express themselves creatively. For those living in a one- or two-room log cabin, a quilt was one of the most important decorative items in a frontier household. R. Carlyle Bulye makes this point in *The Old Northwest: Pioneer Period, 1815–1840:* "Beds were conspicuous objects, in many homes in the main or living room; the [quilt] was a sightly display by day and a warm protector by night."[10]

A quilt began with hundreds of small squares and triangles of cloth. Throughout the winter months, a quilter would piece them together like a jigsaw puzzle to form patterns such as log cabins, windmills, fox, geese, oak leaves, and pine trees. In the warm months these pieces were brought together at a quilting bee, which Christina A. Aubin, on the Quiltersbee.com Web Site, suggests was a major social occasion for the whole community:

> Children were called upon to keep the needles threaded and less skilled quilters and young ladies were often

Making quilts provided frontier women with an outlet for their creativity. In addition to their usefulness as blankets, the quilts served as decorative items in the home.

> relegated to [kitchen] duty, [so] it paid to polish your quilting stitch! . . . At the end of the day the men joined the ladies for a festive supper and perhaps a barn dance. These events were particularly cherished by the women . . . as it was a rare opportunity for them to see other women, [since] they spent most of their days with their own families and chores and might only see others every few months and not at all in the winter. It might be a four or five hour or more journey to the nearest neighbor, a truly perilous trip in winter. Some women were very fussy as to who was invited to a quilting, wanting only the most skilled to work on her quilts.[11]

Weddings and Children

The most festive of all quilting bees were held when a young woman announced her engagement. Tradition dictated that female relatives and friends create up to a dozen quilts at this time, and these were to be only of the highest quality. These bridal quilts were meant to last for decades and were handed down from generation to generation.

Quilting bees were only one part of many great celebrations occasioned by a marriage announcement in the deep woods of the Appalachian wilderness. As Elizabeth F. Ellet writes, weddings were unique events in the life of a frontier community:

> [A] wedding engaged the attention of the whole neighborhood, and the frolic was anticipated by old and young with eager expectation. This will not be wondered at, as a wedding was almost the only gathering unaccompanied with the labor of reaping, log-rolling, building a cabin, or planning some warlike expedition. . . .
>
> [Ladies wore linen] petticoats and . . . coarse shoes, stockings, handkerchiefs, and buckskin gloves, if any. If there were any buckles, rings, buttons, or ruffles, they were the relics of olden times, family pieces from parents or grandparents. . . . The ceremony of the marriage preceded the dinner. . . . During the dinner the greatest hilarity always prevailed. . . . After dinner the dancing commenced, and generally lasted till the next morning. . . . In this way it was often continued till the musician was heartily tired [of] this situation. . . . The feasting and dancing often lasted several days, at the end of which the whole company were so exhausted with the loss of sleep, that

many days' rest was requisite to fit them to return to their ordinary labors.[12]

Women usually became pregnant soon after marriage and were expected to perform their daily chores until it was time to give birth. Babies were delivered at home, in bed. The mother was often surrounded by the other females in the family and aided by an experienced older woman known as a midwife. Doctors were rarely present, and about 25 percent of pioneer women died from childbirth complications such as abnormal bleeding and rupture of the uterus. Mortality was also high among infants, and nearly 50 percent of children died

The Art of the Coverlet

For women weavers, the making of a bedspread, called a coverlet or "kiverlid," was one of the few creative expressions available on the frontier. In *The Old Northwest: Pioneer Period, 1815–1840*, R. Carlyle Buley describes the artistic talents that went into the making of this bedding:

> [The patterns for homemade coverlets] were written on scraps of paper, on old letters, bills, or notes, and passed around as were favorite [recipes]. Most of them were for patterns of geometric figures, but the combinations were varied and pleasing. There were dainty [patterns] . . . irrational patterns, stern and solemn patterns, prim patterns and exuberant patterns—each with its quaint name and its place in history. Curiously, they are like music. They are like little melodies of four notes, full of runs, trills and returns.
>
> With the soft-spun and home-dyed yarns in which indigo blues, madder reds, bronze-blacks, and whites predominated, the weaver dressed the loom and set to work on [patterns with names such as] "Puritan Maiden," "Tennessee Trouble," "Indian War," "Cat Trace," "Snail Trail," "Whig Rose," "Hoosier Beauty," "Gentleman's Fancy," or any of dozens of other patterns. The skillful or practiced weaver possessed a rhythm and touch which was individual. The resulting piece, if not as perfect as the mechanically loomed product, was just as durable and far more charming and satisfying in character; many of these homemade coverlets have remained true to color and intact in fabric, after three generations of use.

before they reached the age of sixteen from common diseases such as scarlet fever, smallpox, and measles.

Romping and Kicking Away Care

Birth and death were just some of the grim realities for women on the frontier. Yet, despite the numerous difficulties, life was not all work and no play. Fun could be found in singing and dancing, or even by turning daily tasks and educational pursuits into contests, as Cathy Luchetti writes in *Home on the Range:*

> Monotony brought about festivity: sleighing parties, spelling bees, literary talks, debates, recitations . . . harvestings, apple peelings. . . . Settlers "danced, sang, romped and . . . kicked away care from morning to night," often riding for fifty miles to attend a dance, with "cakes and party dresses" hung in flour sacks across the saddles. At canning parties, spirits were so high that "nobody ever went home the night they finished." At quilting parties, according to Mayme Reese, the men "ate cold food" until the quilts were finished. Mrs. M.F. Cannon . . . recalled the "barbecues, roundups and dances" of her girlhood, when festive couples might stay all day at a picnic, stop on the way home at a house, and dance until morning to the music of fiddles.[13]

While frontier life could be fun, frightening, or just plain hard work, pioneer women rarely sat still. From the moment they awoke to the time they went to bed, women performed dozens of difficult daily tasks unimaginable to modern Americans. Through hard work and perseverance pioneer women created comfortable homes for themselves and their families in the wilderness of the American frontier.

Chapter 2: Army Wives and Camp Followers

Life on the American frontier was difficult for most women, but those who were married to military men faced special hardships. Army wives were forced to endure not just primitive living conditions but frequent moves, often to territory where hostilities between whites and Native Americans posed the real possibility of death.

Many army wives lived at isolated forts where the most unpleasant conditions prevailed. Those residing at bases such as Fort Rice in the Dakota Territory suffered from bone-chilling cold and months of isolation as snowdrifts buried their tents. Women whose husbands were stationed in places such as Fort Yuma, Arizona, spent their days under a blistering sun fending off biting insects and stifling boredom.

The suffering of army wives was compounded when husbands left for months at a time to fight Indian wars or practice military maneuvers. There was often no mail, telegraph, or other means of communication. As a consequence, wives did not know if their husbands were dead or alive. As Elizabeth "Libbie" Custer, wife of General George Custer, wrote (shortly before her husband was killed in battle in 1876) military wives are "prey to all the horrors of imagining what may be happening to [the] one we love. You slowly eat your heart out with anxiety, and to endure such suspense is simply the hardest of all the trials that come to a soldier's wife."[14]

Camp Followers

To add to their miseries, the wives of officers and enlisted men were accorded little status by the military. Army regulations referred to wives as "camp followers," a term that was also applied to the prostitutes who set up brothels close to most forts. Other camp followers were unmarried women who took on the roles of cooks, laundresses, housekeepers, and nurses, among other jobs. Except for laundresses, who were considered essential, most camp followers were subject to the whims of the post's commanding officer. Most army wives, even those of officers, could be ordered to leave the fort at any time by the commander. Despite their inferior status, these women played important roles in the day-to-day lives of military men. According to Glenda Riley in *The Female Frontier:*

> [Army] wives, daughters, and sisters fulfilled their domestic tasks and duties under difficult conditions. Despite minimally furnished kitchens and limited provisions from the fort commissary, they not only cooked for their own families but also carried out the entertaining, baking, and charity work that was expected from them among the poorer families in and around the fort.
>
> Of all the women's jobs, child care was probably the most challenging in the midst of the dangers and privations of a frontier fort. Women served as children's mothers, nursemaids, playmates, and teachers.[15]

Courage and Ability to Survive

For the wives of officers, their low status in the eyes of the military contrasted sharply with their experience in civilian life. In those days, military officers generally came from socially prominent families, and their wives did as well. These women often had grown up in fancy houses where slaves or servants catered to their every need. When they arrived at military forts, however, they quickly realized that they were only as important as their husband's rank. As Martha Summerhayes wrote from Camp Apache in the Arizona Territory: "I soon discovered that however much education, position and money might count in civil life, *rank* seemed to be the one and only thing in the army, and [my husband] Jack had not much of that just then."[16]

Housing was allocated by a soldier's rank, and at crowded forts, even higher-ranking officers were not offered much in the way of quarters. In these places, living space was given a lower priority than ammunition storage and other military uses. Army wives might find that their new home was a filthy old tent, a converted chicken coop, or even a pit dug into the hillside. In many of these structures, the wind whistled through cracks, roofs leaked, and floors were so damp that in warm weather toadstools might pop up overnight. Furniture was anything that could be thrown together with materials on hand. Tables, chairs, and beds were made from old wooden packing crates, barrels, slabs of wood, and itchy, wool army blankets. Such dwellings were infested with all manner of unpleasant creatures, from lice and chiggers to skunks and weasels. As Anne Bruner Eales writes in *Army Wives on the*

Following Orders

In the nineteenth century, military men vying for promotion were judged by their wives' actions as well as their own. For this reason, some officers imposed strict regulations at home. In *Army Wives on the American Frontier,* Anne Bruner Eales reproduces a list of guidelines one unnamed army colonel required his young bride to observe:

1. You will see that meals are served on time.
2. You will not come to the table in a wrapper [robe].
3. You will smile at breakfast.
4. If possible, you will serve meat four times a week.
5. You will not move the furniture without my permission.
6. You will present the household accounts to me by the fifth of each month.
7. You will examine my uniforms every Tuesday and, if they need repair, you will take the necessary action.
8. You will do no work in the evenings. You will entertain me.
9. You will not touch my desk.
10. You will remember you are not in command of anything except the [hired] cook.

American Frontier, such conditions forced women to abandon their roles as prim nineteenth-century housewives and confront new hardships with ingenuity and bravery:

> Wives who had been unwilling to remove a dead mouse from a trap in the East encountered rattlesnakes on their mantels, tarantulas in their kitchens, and bats hanging from the blankets on their beds. Women went hungry as food shipments were delayed by Indian attacks; they were buried in avalanches in Montana and trapped in quicksand in Nebraska. Army wives gave birth in the back of unsprung wagons with only a stranger to help them and then protected those children with a bull-whip or a pistol. They brained wolves with skillets and shot buffalo while riding sidesaddle on a galloping horse.[17]

Brightening Up a Home

Ingenuity was a necessary attribute for army wives. Officers had to move often, and the army allowed them to bring only one thousand pounds of baggage for himself and his family. Anything over that weight had to be shipped at a rate of $2 per hundred pounds—a large sum when an officer's pay averaged less than $150 a month. For this reason, women had to be experts at packing efficiently. For example, Martha Summerhayes learned to pack her family's belongings into only three large army chests, rolling carpets and bedding to fit inside. Others formulated clever designs for "composite" furniture. Elizabeth Custer had post carpenters build packing crates that doubled as a base for a long couch. She also designed moving chests with shelves that were covered in calico cloth and used as dressers at the next destination. Like pioneer women on the Appalachian frontier, she saved scraps of cloth that were woven into rag rugs. Her material had a decidedly military bent, however. One rug was made of blue from her husband's officer pants, yellow from the trim of his cavalry rider's uniform, and black from a military widow's mourning veil.

Frontier military officers and their families typically lived in crude cabins like this, and military wives used scraps of cloth, clothing, and even old cannons to decorate them.

The wives of enlisted men did not have luxuries like those enjoyed by Elizabeth Custer. They still managed to brighten up homes for their families, however. Windows were covered with muslin cloth curtains that were dyed red with beet juice. Nails in the walls were utilized to hang clothes; dirt floors were covered with hay, blankets, and newspapers. Elizabeth Burt even found a way to use military hardware in her household at Fort Leavenworth, Kansas. The centerpiece of the Burt dining room—which was a former ammunitions storage room—was an old cannon that was straddled as a seat or surrounded by benches for use as a dining table during mealtime.

Many military wives also became amateur gardeners, utilizing the bright ornamentation provided by native shrubs and flowers. These plants could be picked in the nearby countryside and planted around military housing to add cheer to otherwise dull structures.

Wives had to be careful about making a dwelling too comfortable, however. If a senior officer visited and liked what he saw, he could "rank out" the family of a subordinate, ordering them out of the quarters and taking it over for himself. For example, when the wife of a junior officer at Fort Davis, Texas, installed a bathtub in her family's quarters, they were ranked out by a senior officer. Women did not necessarily accept such treatment without a fight, however. When Lieutenant Frank Baldwin ranked out the family of Lieutenant William Foulk, at Fort Harker, Kansas, Mrs. Foulk attacked Baldwin with a horsewhip while her children pummeled him with books.

Feeding the Family

Like all other women in the nineteenth century, army wives were expected to be cooks. Women at military posts, however, were forced to assume that role with much less in the way of resources. As was true everywhere on the frontier, there were no stores, butchers, or farmers' markets, and foodstuffs such as eggs, butter, and milk were always in short supply. In fact, a traveler wanting to present a military wife with a luxury item might carefully pack a few eggs as a precious gift. In some places, food shortages were so severe that women and children survived for years on army rations that consisted of small portions of bacon, flour, beans, coffee, rice, and sugar. When an occasional wagon full of food was brought to a fort, prices were extremely high, with a bushel of potatoes selling for $15—about 30 percent of a lower-ranking officer's monthly pay.

High prices and food shortages forced many formerly prim and proper ladies to become farmers. As Anne Bruner Eales writes:

> The shortage of poultry and the cost of up to $2.50 a dozen for eggs inspired women, whose eastern experience with animals had largely been limited to riding horses or petting dogs and cats, to become "chicken farmers." . . . Ellen Biddle went into business at [Arizona's] Fort Whipple and eventually sold more than 200 chickens and 14 turkeys. Mrs. D.B. Dyer raised over 250 chickens her first year at Fort Reno, Oklahoma Territory. She discovered that feeding them sunflower seeds produced extremely shiny feathers, making the birds look healthier. Fannie Boyd kept chickens and cows, selling enough butter and eggs to save fifty dollars a month, almost half of her husband's income for the same period. Of course there was an added risk to business "stock" in the West. The Carringtons drove two milk cows six hundred miles to a new post only to have the animals stolen by Indians soon after their arrival. Then wolves ate their turkey hen just when she was preparing to hatch a brood of future merchandise.[18]

Fruits and vegetables were also difficult to obtain on the frontier, and vegetable farming was often not easy for army wives. Much of the western frontier was arid, and often the soil was poor. Rabbit, grasshoppers, and other creatures ravaged crops that did grow. Even if growing conditions were right, there was no guarantee that one might be around to harvest a crop, since soldiers were often reassigned, forcing their wives to abandon their gardens. One wife, whose husband was in the cavalry, planted gardens for twelve years but never remained at one location long enough to harvest the produce when the growing season was over.

Where farming was difficult, some army wives learned to hunt in order to provide relief from army rations. Women shot buffalo, deer, rabbit, game birds, and even bears and mountain goats. Ellen Biddle found a particularly unusual way to provide fish for her family. She requested that officers set off dynamite in a nearby river. The resulting explosion caused hundreds of fish to rain down on the nearby banks. The resulting "catch" most likely fed dozens of hungry soldiers for days.

Laundresses

While army wives spent their days trying to provide food and comfort for their husbands and families, other camp followers worked directly for the military. These were the laundresses who scrubbed the filthy clothes of soldiers.

Beginning in 1802, regulations stated that the army should hire enough laundresses to number one for every seventeen men assigned to a post. Regulations provided laundresses and each one of their children with one ration of food per day, although this may have only consisted of a meager offering of meat, bread, and whiskey. The washerwomen also received bedding straw and, when necessary, were entitled to be treated by the post surgeon. Laundresses were not paid by individuals. Instead, their pay was deducted from soldiers' wages and then given to them by the fort paymaster. At most forts, laundresses were paid fifty cents per month for each soldier assigned to them. In addition a laundress was paid two dollars for a single officer, and four dollars for a married officer and his family. With this pay scale, a laundress could earn more than forty dollars a month—about three times what an army private earned.

Despite being considered essential, these women were only granted the poorest housing. Laundresses lived in tents, shanties, and dugouts located on "Suds Row" or "Soapsuds Row." On nearly every military post, this ramshackle row of housing was located as far as possible from the main parade ground. Soapsuds Row was notorious for its hoards of crying children and barking dogs. Little wonder that the laundresses were described by one unnamed general as "red armed wives . . . with broods

Making Do with Less

Women who lived on military bases had to cook with poor quality foods supplied at the fort food store, or commissary. As Cathy Luchetti writes in *Home on the Range*, army wives drew on their ingenuity and creativity to make decent meals from a limited supply of provisions:

> Military wives accustomed to the nicety of a clean, well-supplied kitchen [in civilian life] viewed the commissary rations with dismay. What could be done with such dull soldier's fare? Doors and larders were opened to each other in easy companionableness, and the women shared recipes and spices to lend some daintiness to such crudities as boiled tripe. Delicate slices of preserved [lemonlike] citron masked the smell of rancid oil in cakes; moldy potatoes were sliced and baked as [potato] chips, or airy potato puffs. Artistic conscience ruled the larder as bacon, flour, beans . . . coffee, tea, rice, sugar, and dried apples were laid out with attention to presentation. Some women bought cows or chickens from local ranchers, hauling them from post to post.

of unkempt urchins who raced around the big black laundry kettles that bubbled over wood fires in the backyards of Suds Row shanties."[19]

Despite this description, laundresses who were single were highly attractive to lonely soldiers stationed at forts. A private lucky enough to marry a laundress could move out of the barracks and raise a family on Suds Row with a woman who earned more than most men of that era did. These soldiers, however, were often considered useless by the army. In 1876, Captain Henry G. Thomas complained to a congressional committee that the soldier-husbands of laundresses constantly requested leave to stay at home and take care of their children while the wives washed clothes.

Witnesses to Suffering and War

Whether a laundress or an officer's wife, many women associated with the army were as dedicated to the military as the men were. In numerous cases, women performed bravely and selflessly when duty called. When the Seventh Cavalry was stationed near Yankton, South Dakota, in 1873, a late April blizzard stranded Elizabeth Custer, her husband, and several others. Eales describes how Custer helped assure the survival of the men trapped with her:

> While caring for her sick husband, Libbie struggled to provide for half a dozen soldiers who straggled in from the storm, keep everyone from freezing to death, and obtain enough food for all to survive. Because she had no liquor to warm the troops, she gave them the alcohol normally used in the little spirit lamps, a form of camp stove, and wrapped the men in carpets intended for her quarters. Only after the snow ended and rescuers arrived did Libbie break down.[20]

While fighting nature, many army wives also lived in constant fear of Indian attacks. As the U. S. Army built more than 110 forts on the frontier between 1860 and 1875, Native Americans in many areas often responded violently to the intruders on their lands. Women who lived in such forts were sometimes witnesses to hideous acts of war that left them in great despair. Many experienced what would be described today as symptoms of posttraumatic stress disorder—insomnia, depression, fear, anxiety, and emotional outbursts. For example, Frances Grummond, wife of Lieutenant Colonel George Grummond, traveled to Fort Kearny, in northern Wyoming Territory in 1866. Upon her arrival, she witnessed a wagon entering the fort carrying the naked body of a soldier who

In 1873 a blizzard stranded Elizabeth Custer (right), her husband George (left), and other soldiers at a South Dakota camp. During their confinement, Elizabeth provided for everyone's needs.

had been scalped and mutilated by Cheyenne warriors. After witnessing additional macabre spectacles in the months that followed, Grummond experienced depression and even considered suicide.

Grummond's fears were well founded: Indian attacks occurred in and around Fort Kearny fifty-one times in the following months, often within the sight of women and children. During this time Margaret Carrington, wife of post commander Colonel Henry Carrington, wrote that she observed "men shot within thirty yards of the gates . . . and saw five wagonloads of bodies"[21] enter the fort. At one point, fearing Indians would attack and overrun the fort, Colonel Carrington instructed officers to hide the women and children among the ammunition stores, supplied with bread, crackers, water, and other surplus foods. He further ordered, "[In] the event of a last desperate struggle, [kill them] all together, rather than have them captured alive."[22] Such orders caused the women to live in a constant state of anxiety and fear.

Grummond's husband was eventually killed in an ambush near the fort. His throat was slit, he had been scalped, his fingers were removed, and his body was filled with bullets and arrows. Grummond described her state of grief after the remains of her husband were returned to the fort:

> And then [came] the horrors of the following days, the making of coffins and digging in the hard, frozen earth for a burial place, when the cold was so intense that the men worked in fifteen-minute reliefs, and a guard was constantly on the alert lest Indians should interrupt. . . . One half of the headquarters building, which was my temporary home, was unfinished, and this part was utilized by carpenters for making pine cases for the dead. I knew that my husband's coffin was being made, and the sound of hammers and the grating of saws was torture.[23]

Grieving and Homeless

Grummond's grief was compounded when the army ordered her to leave the base. Like all other army wives whose husbands had been killed, Grummond and her children lost all rights to claim food and shelter from the military. Grummond, and those in her situation, were obligated to take what little money they had and find new homes for themselves and their children. This was particularly difficult for women who were thousands of miles away from friends and family.

The burden of a military spouse's death was compounded because the army did not pay for transportation of a fallen soldier's body home, nor for his funeral. Sometimes the body had to be moved hundreds of miles from a battlefield to a widow's home. For example, when Mary Clarke's husband, Frank, died in Tennessee from disease during the Civil War in 1863, Mary was living at the isolated Fort Riley in Kansas. Since she supported herself running a ferry business on the nearby Kansas

River, she wanted to stay in the area. In a letter to her mother, Mary describes the hardship imposed by having to transport her husband's body back from Tennessee for burial at Fort Riley's military cemetery:

> I had to pay for everything. Government gave me no transportation for anything either his corpse, or effects, or horse. I had to pay for all, or [his remains might stay in Tennessee] if I was not able to do so. There is no such thing allowed as transportation to an officer. I did not ask for anything. I had enough to pay my way but if I had not it was all the same.[24]

Sympathy for the Natives

Even as the U.S. Army was in the process of confiscating the ancestral lands from Native Americans, some of the women living at forts expressed compassion for the plight of the Indians. In *The Female Frontier*, Glenda Riley quotes several army wives who expressed feelings of sympathy for the indigenous people:

> A number of plainswomen sharply criticized [military] actions toward Indians. . . . Army wife Frances Roe . . . came to believe that there was blatant injustice involved in the mass killing of buffalo which deprived the Plains Indians of their primary source of support. She wrote scathingly, "If the Indians should attempt to protect their rights it would be called an uprising at once, so they have to lie around on sand hills and watch their beloved buffalo gradually disappear, and all the time they know only too well that with them will go the skins that give them tepees and clothing, and the meat that furnishes almost all of their sustenance." Another army wife was even more adamant concerning the unfairness of seizing the precious resources that were so crucial to native populations. While at Fort Laramie during the 1860s, Frances Carrington observed that "at the time of my arrival it had become apparent to any sensible observer that the Indians of that country would fight to the death for home and native land, with spirit akin to that of the American soldier of our early history, and who could say that their spirit was not commendable and to be respected."

A Very Pleasant Community

Despite the ever-present possibility of being widowed, many army wives managed to make the best of their circumstances. Army wives organized theatrical companies and put on plays to rooms crowded with soldiers grateful for the diversion. Others sang, danced, or played musical instruments. Holidays were often marked with balls and celebrations. And in places where there were no hostilities, some women spent their days riding horseback and exploring the beauties of the western countryside. As renowned artist George Catlin wrote in 1833 about the women at Fort Leavenworth, in Kansas:

> In this delightful [place], the presence of officers' wives and daughters create a very pleasant little community who are almost continually together in social enjoyment of the peculiar amusements and pleasures of this wild country . . . riding on horseback or in carriages . . . picking strawberries and wild plums, deer hunting, grouse shooting, horse racing and other amusements.[25]

Freed from the strict conventions of nineteenth-century life, army wives and camp followers assumed roles that would have been denied them had they married civilians. While the hardships were many, as Sandra L. Myers wrote in *Western Historical Quarterly*, "The more independent and less restrained the lives [the women] lived in the West made [them] more aware of their own assets and abilities and made them more willing to step outside the 'woman's [traditional] place'"[26] in society.

Chapter 3: Women on the Trail

In the early decades of the nineteenth century, a few hundred trappers and traders made their way to the Pacific Northwest on a rough path known as the Oregon Trail. Some of them settled in the Willamette Valley, near present-day Salem, Oregon. In 1843, using powers granted to them by the U.S. Congress, 102 citizens of the Willamette Valley drafted Oregon's first constitution, called the Organic Act. Section seventeen of the act, which covered present-day Oregon, Washington, and parts of Idaho, granted 640 acres of free land to every male settler or married couple. An additional 160 acres were offered to the settlers for each child in the family.

The Organic Act set off a land rush known as Oregon Fever, which prompted thousands of people to load their possessions into covered wagons and head to the new frontier. Their main route was the Oregon Trail, also known as the Emigrant or Overland Trail. This primitive path wound nearly twenty-four hundred miles from Independence, Missouri, through the Great Plains, the Rocky Mountains, and the parched deserts west of the Rockies. In what came to be known as the Great Migration, more than three hundred thousand men, women, and children traveled the Oregon Trail between 1840 and 1869.

A Decidedly Different Outlook

Many of the men who traveled the Oregon Trail were motivated by the promise of riches in the form of free land and a seemingly inexhaustible supply of animal furs, which had great value in the East. These men looked at the journey as a grand adventure to be taken in the prime years of their lives. Women, however, had a decidedly different outlook. About one in five female travelers was pregnant, and almost all married women were migrating with small children in their care. This left them extremely vulnerable, causing Catherine Haun to write in 1849 that she was "dazed with dread"[27] when contemplating the dangers inherent in the long journey. Haun was not alone. Many women wrote with great anguish about the difficult decision to leave family, friends, and familiar surroundings. And once the journey was completed, few had the resources to return home, even if they so desired. As poverty-stricken Martha Minto wrote from Oregon City in 1850, "We had no horses, not cattle, or anything to haul us [back] across the plains; we had no provisions; we could not [return] naked and destitute in every way."[28]

Despite the harsh realities of the Great Migration, some women were risk takers who looked forward to the adventure. For example, Sarah J. Cummins wrote in 1845, "We were surely taking a wild and inconsiderate step for we had no definite knowledge of our [fate], and yet we were willing and anxious to plunge into the . . . wild and risk the dangers that were so numerous with no definite knowledge of what might lie [ahead]."[29]

Many other women undertook the journey only because they were expected to play the roles of dutiful wives—their husbands had decided the family would go and, in that era, a husband had the final say. As Abby E. Fulkerath wrote after immigrating to Oregon—and seeing several of her children die on the trail: "[Submitting] to the wish of my husband, I left all my relatives in Ohio . . . & started on this long & . . . perilous journey. . . . It proved a hard task to leave them but still harder to leave my chil-

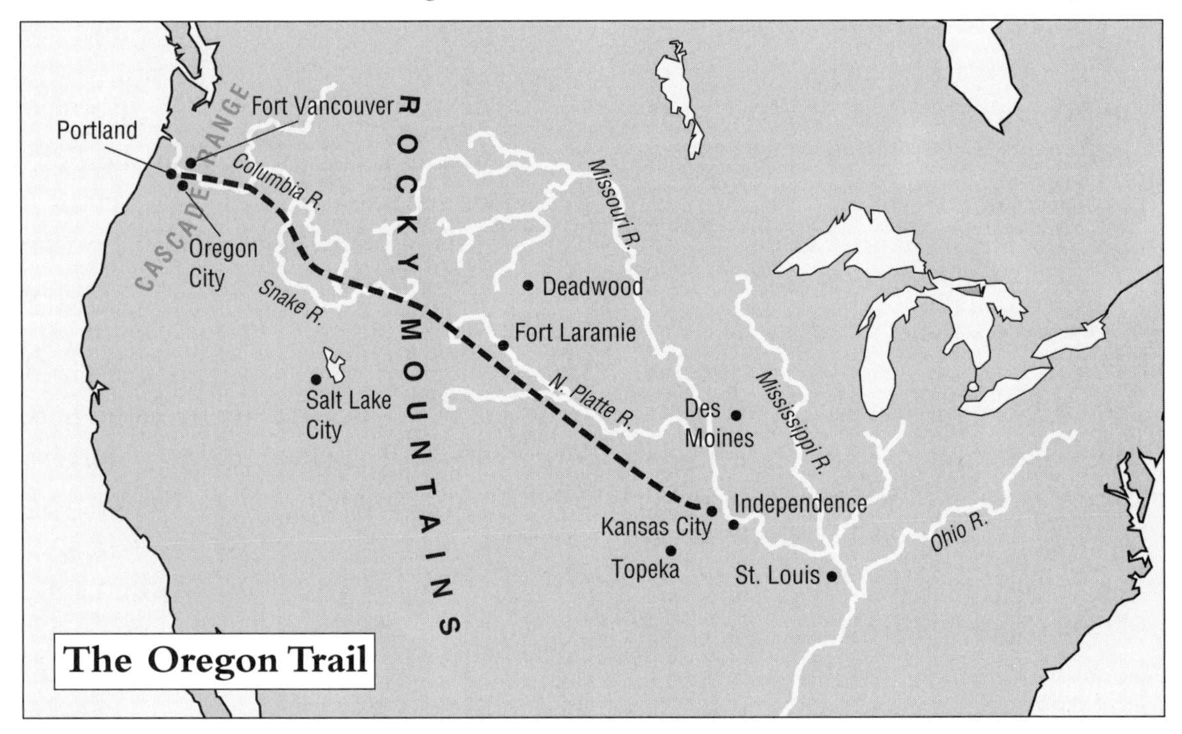

dren buried in . . . graveyards [along the way]."[30]

"The Pain of Leaving"

Those who made the Great Migration faced hardships that were barely imaginable to those who stayed home. There were no maps, and the guidebooks of the era were wildly inaccurate in their statements regarding the conditions the travelers might expect. Wagon trains traveled very slowly, moving at the speed of what one woman said was that of a funeral procession. The trail was carved into the banks of rivers and streams, and paths were deeply rutted and muddy. Immigrants were forced to cross deep, fast-flowing rivers dozens of times.

Based on exaggerated stories, immigrants worried constantly about being murdered by Indians. But in reality, over the twenty-six years that the trail saw the heaviest traffic, only 362 settlers total were killed by Indians. On the other hand, immigrants killed 426 Native Americans. Indians were, however, known to attack the immigrants without warning, stealing supplies, driving off horses and cattle, or kidnapping women and holding them for ransom in the form of money, tools, guns, horses, liquor, and other supplies. A bigger killer was the weather, which could deliver searing heat, rain, lightning, hail, snow, and bitter cold—sometimes all within a single day.

Accidents, disease, and disaster lurked around every bend of the Oregon Trail. Travelers spent their days walking past dead cattle, overturned wagons, and abandoned possessions. One unnamed woman described the scene: "On the bluffs above the Platte [River] you can look back at the wide seas of grass sloping this way and that, at the wide, dry sea of America strewn with the discards: food, bedding, clothes, trunks full of ball dresses, books, furniture, machinery—everything, in fact."[31]

Women also noted the shallow graves of those who, like them, had once dreamed of riches on the western frontier. Susan G. Butruille describes the harsh realities of the Great Migration in *Women's Voices from the Oregon Trail:*

> [Women's] diaries recorded the pain of leaving. Counting the miles by the graves of cholera and accident victims. Burying the dead and then driving wagons over the grave to hide the body from wolves. . . . The stench of animal carcasses along the alkali water country of Wyoming. Skull-deadening boredom. The heartbreak of separation on the trail as families either lost track of one another or chose to go separate ways. Struggling to keep some semblance of "civilization" on the trail

against the uncivilizing intrusions of dust and mud and water and bugs and blood and vomit. Facing starvation after following bad advice to take an untried cutoff. Children falling from wagons. Husbands drowning in river crossings or dying from accidental gunshot wounds. Giving birth on the trail and relying on the comfort and help of other women. Struggling to keep from giving in to emotions, fearing insanity. At the end of the journey, the woman's recognition that she would never again be the same person who left her home many months and miles ago.[32]

Under these circumstances women on the trail had to assume many roles simply to survive. They were wagon drivers, hunters, doctors, midwifes, and "janes-of-all-trades." They did whatever was necessary to keep their families alive and moving west.

Preparing for Survival

The hard work began long before a family set foot upon the Oregon Trail. While the trip was still being planned, women were called upon to use their weaving skills to make the billowing, white top for the covered wagon. As Kit Belknap wrote in 1848: "[The] first thing is to make a piece of linen for a wagon cover . . . [I] will spin most evenings while my husband reads to me."[33]

The hard part of the journey began after traveling by train, horse, and riverboat to Independence, Missouri, or some other jumping-off place. But before setting off on the trail itself, immigrants needed to gather supplies and prepare their wagons. As men spent their days buying livestock and building wagons, women were in charge of gathering foodstuffs. Travel guides at that time recommended that a woman purchase—for a family of four for a four- to six-month trip—eight hundred pounds of flour, two hundred pounds of hard bread or crackers, three hundred pounds of bacon, one hundred pounds of dried apples, one hundred pounds of sugar, forty pounds of coffee, fifty pounds of rice, and about ten pounds of salt and pepper.

After the food was obtained, women were called upon to organize and somehow pack the food, along with all the family's belongings, into a wagon ten feet long, four feet wide, and two feet deep. Supplies had to be stowed so that a woman could continue to cook and clean for the family out on the trail without having to unload the wagon each time. Belknap describes her packing method with an eye toward making meals homey:

"Made Me a Fine Tent"

In late summer 1854 the amazingly spry seventy-four-year-old Tabitha Brown was separated from her party and left alone with an even older person, the retired sea captain John Brown who was in his eighties. Tabitha found herself in the unenviable position of having to make camp and take care of the ailing Captain Brown. In a letter to her brother and sister, reprinted in Kenneth L. Holmes's *Covered Wagon Women*, she explains how she made due in her dilemma:

> The sun was . . . setting, the wind was blowing, and the rain was drifting, upon the side of distant mountains—poor Me! . . . I alighted from my horse, flung off my saddle and saddle bags, and tied him fast with a las[so] rope to a tree. The Captain asked what I was going to do. My answer was, I am going to camp for the night. He gave a groan, and fell to the ground. I gathered my wagon sheet, that I had put under my saddle; flung it over a firm projecting limb of a tree, and made me a fine tent. I then stripped the Captain's horse, and tied him; placed saddles, blankets, bridles, etc. under the tent; then helped up the bewildered old gentleman, and introduced him to his new lodgings upon the naked ground. His senses were gone; I covered him as well as I could with blankets, and then seated myself upon my feet behind him, expecting he would be a corpse by morning. Pause for a moment and consider my situation—worse than alone; in a strange wilderness; without food, without fire; cold and shivering; wolves fighting and howling all around me; darkness of night forbade the stars to shine upon me; solitary—all was solitary as death.

[I pack] the groceries. We will make a wall of smaller sacks stood on end; dried apples and peaches, beans, rice, sugar and coffee, the latter being in the green state. We will brown it in a skillet as we want to use it. Everything must be put in strong bags; no paper wrappings for the trip. There is a corner left for the wash-tub and the lunch basket will just fit in the tub. The dishes we want to use will all be in the basket. I am going to start with good earthen dishes and if they get broken have tin ones to take their place. Have made nice little table cloths so am going to live just like I was at home.[34]

"Unladylike Labor"

Despite efficient packing, these wagons—known as prairie schooners because their white covers resembled a ship's sails—had to be packed and unpacked repeatedly. The wagons were prone to becoming mired in axle-deep mud and could only be freed after being completely emptied. The cloth coverings did not prevent heavy rains from dousing clothing, bedding, and other goods which then had to be unpacked and laid out in the sun—or near a campfire—to dry.

In many places, the muddy trail went up—or down—extremely steep hills, and women were pressed into service, helping to maneuver the wagons. When heading downhill, travelers tried to brake their wagons by cutting pine trees and tying the bushy branches to the wheels to drag on the ground and slow the descent. Then, according to Catherine Haun:

> A rope or chain would be tied to the rear of the wagon and every one, man, woman and child would be pressed into service to hold the wagon back. [To go up steep hills] a chain or rope would be fastened to the front axle and we climbed up impossible bowlders and pulled with might and main while the men pushed with herculanian strength. . . . Many times the greater part of the day would be consumed in this strenuous and altogether unladylike labor. . . . And oh, such pulling, pushing, tugging it was![35]

Women were also called upon to be wranglers, wrestling the oxen in and out of the yokes that were attached to the wagon. In 1844 thirteen-year-old Martha Morris wrote that "some women did nearly all of the yoking; many times the men were off. One time my father was away hunting cattle that had been driven off by the Indians, and that left mother and three children to attend to everything."[36]

While some men were physically absent, others suffered mental breakdowns as a result of the labor, sickness, and fear of Indian attack. When this happened, women had no choice but to take charge. According to author Eliza G. Farnham in *California, In-doors and Out*, when one unnamed woman's husband broke "under the tremendous sufferings of that terrible journey [she became] the efficient care-taker of him and their three sons; yoked and unyoked the oxen, gathered fuel, cooked their food . . . and for months performed all the coarser offices that properly belonged to the other sex."[37]

"Feminine Occupations"

In addition to other chores, women had to cook out on the open prairie. Women often varied their families' diets with some of the natural abundance found along the Oregon Trail. Wild turkey, quail, prairie chickens, doves, and pheasant were but a few types of fowl easily shot on the prairie. Rivers flashed with trout, bluegill, and other fish. Farther west, wild strawberries, gooseberries, and cranberries improved meals. And the prairies were thick with millions of buffalo, whose meat compared favorably to beef.

Buffalo also provided women with another element essential for cooking: fuel. To make dinner, a woman would dig a fire pit and fill it with dried buffalo dung, referred to as "chips" or "prairie coal." For many women, this polite name did little to overcome their aversion to using it, although the coal burned very hot and did not emit much of an odor. In 1864 Arabella Clemens Fulton described the reaction of her sisters—and herself—to this abundant fuel:

> Here was the summer range of the buffalo, and we cooked with buffalo "chips." When we camped at evening, the women and children went out with sacks and gathered the chips with which we cooked our meals. . . . When we first began using this improvised fuel my sisters couldn't eat anything; their delicate appetites revolted at food prepared in this manner. But before we left the chip country they were only too glad to get food, regardless of how it had been cooked, and they later saw times when they would gladly have cooked with chips had they been able to get them. I had no qualms about such things, and I could gather chips for fuel, cook with them, and eat heartily and poke fun at the girls over their squeamish appetites.[38]

Once the buffalo chips were kindled into smoldering embers, meat could be cooked in a frying pan and bread baked in a covered pan called a Dutch oven. A canvas cloth or blanket spread on the ground served as a dining room table, brightened by a centerpiece of a few wild prairie flowers in a tin cup. After dinner, women went to the nearest river where they scoured their soot-blackened utensils with sand and gravel.

In addition to washing dishes, women took on the task of promoting cleanliness, which the men would have chosen to do without. As Fulton writes:

> I remember the Wood River and the delightful camping spot it afforded us; also the washing and clean up with which the women kept up their habits of cleanliness on every practicable occasion was remarkable.

> We found so many nice, clear streams of soft water that the men complained about so much washing, saying the women were forever wanting to stop and wash. They argued that, since we traveled in dust, cooked and ate in dust, slept in dust and dirt, and were in it all the time, why should we go to the trouble of washing and cleaning so often?
>
> It did seem futile, and we could not give a good reason for so much washing, except that it was a habit and a desire to see the children clean, and to feel clean ourselves once in a while. Further, we said, we were not stopping any too often for the good of the stock. This last argument was a clincher. Our whole dependence was on our animals, and some of them were getting very thin, worn, and weary, and so much in need of rest.[39]

After bathing and washing clothes, a woman might lead her children in song, read a story out loud by the light of a campfire, or dance to a tune played on a fiddle or a guitar by another traveler. The next morning at first light, travel resumed. When there were no emergencies, women fell into a routine, as described by Catherine Haun:

> During the day we womenfolk visited from wagon to wagon or congenial friends spent an hour walking, ever westward, and talking over our home life back in "the states" telling of the loved ones left behind; voicing our hopes for the future in the far west and even whispering a little friendly gossip of emigrant life.
>
> High teas were not popular but tatting [making lace], knitting, crocheting, exchanging [recipes] for cooking beans or dried apples or swapping food for the sake of variety kept us in practice of feminine occupations and diversions.[40]

Nursing the Sick

If childcare, cooking, and cleaning were the province of women along the Oregon Trail, so was nursing the wounded, sick, and dying. There was plenty of nursing to do since cholera, a highly infectious disease of the digestive tract, reached epidemic proportions between 1849 and 1854. The uncontrollable diarrhea and vomiting resulted in severe dehydration that was often fatal, sometimes within hours. As one unnamed traveler wrote, cholera was not apt to last long: "[There] was no case of lingering suffering. When attacked, a single day ordinarily ended the strife in death or recovery."[41]

Along the Oregon Trail, a woman gathers buffalo dung for use as fuel. Despite the aversion of many women to cooking with dung, it was the only fuel available on the Great Plains.

There was no medicine that could cure cholera or many of the other diseases that stalked travelers, including dysentery, measles, typhoid, smallpox, and scarlet fever. In some cases home remedies might have some curative power—or could at least ease the pain. Haun writes that she brought along medicines such as "quinine for malaria, hartshorn [an herb] for snakebites, citric acid for scurvy, and opium and whiskey for everything else."[42] Elizabeth Geer wrote that "no one should travel this road without medicine. . . . Each family should have a box of physicking [purging] pills, a quart of castor oil, a quart of the best rum, and a large vial of peppermint essence."[43]

When the efforts at a cure failed and the victim died, often there were orphaned children. In such cases, other women would take the youngsters in. Catherine Sager's father was crushed to death in a buffalo stampede, and then her mother, who had recently given birth, was overcome with a deadly illness called "camp fever." Sager writes: "[Mother] soon became delirious. . . .

Her babe was cared for by the women of the [wagon] train. The kind-hearted women were also in the habit of coming in when the train stopped at night to wash the dust from [mother's] face and other wise make her comfortable."[44] Sager's mother soon died, leaving seven children as orphans, the youngest only a few weeks old, the oldest fourteen. The children were cared for by other women in the wagon train. According to Lillian Schlissel, by taking on such roles as nurses and guardians, women developed a different perspective from men:

> As ritual caretakers of the sick and the dying, the women saw the real enemies of the road as disease and accident. . . . The women knew that disease and accident killed more emigrants than did Indians. The women, whose job it was to care for the dying, carefully noted the cost of the westward movement in human life. Whereas men recorded the death in aggregate numbers, the women knew death as personal catastrophe and noted the particulars of each grave site, whether it was newly dug or old, whether of a young person or an adult, whether it had been disturbed by wolves or by Indians. The women . . . [counted] the miles with the lives that were lost.[45]

For some who survived the cross-country journey, the dream of striking it rich on the western frontier may have seemed a bitter joke. The land was beau-

Many pioneers died from cholera and other virulent diseases along the Oregon Trail. In addition to their other duties, frontier women had the difficult job of nursing the sick and dying.

tiful—and cheap—but life was very difficult for women who had lost husbands out on the trail. As the ten-year-old Elvina Apperson Fellows writes about her family's trip:

> We came . . . over the Cascades . . . and it was a fierce route. The oldest child . . . had died before we started, and father died on the way across the plains, so when we reached Portland our family consisted of my mother and nine children.
>
> Mother had no money and had nine hungry mouths to feed in addition to her own, so she would go to the ships that came [in] and get washing to do.[46]

"The Wonderful Panorama of Beauty"

For all the hard work and troubles women endured on the way west, remarkably, a few found time to keep detailed diaries. While this might have seemed like an unimportant task at the time, the sensitive descriptions of the journey, its hardships, and its beauties have informed, saddened, and delighted succeeding generations for more than a century and a half. Historians have been able to use these letters and journals to piece together an accurate picture of what daily life was like for those who settled the West.

The optimism of discovery and the joy in the natural beauty that these diarists express is remarkable considering the adversity under which some journals were written. While Sarah Cummins was lost on Mount Hood in the Cascade Mountains of Oregon, pouring rain turned to blinding snow as food supplies dwindled. Soaking wet, freezing, and suffering from exposure, Cummins and her party searched the rocky mountaintop for firewood. After great difficulty, a fire was started that began to thaw her frozen limbs. Cummins later recorded that such excruciating "pains seized me that I was wild with pain and could not forbear the scream that rent the air on that wild mountain."[47] In spite of her pain and hunger, Cummins awoke the next day and decided to climb a nearby summit to get a view of her anticipated home in the valley below. The suffering of the previous day forgotten, Cummins's poetic lyricism reaches across generations to describe a primeval forest that would soon disappear under the axes of countless settlers:

> The sky was cloudless. The storms of the previous day had so cleared the air of dust and impurities that my horizon was boundless, and this, my first, prospect of everlasting green

Women as Diarists

People of both genders recorded their thoughts on the long walk west. But as Lillian Schlissel writes in *Women's Diaries of the Westward Journey*, there was a distinct difference between the observations of men and those of women:

> [Men write] of fight, conflict and competition and . . . hunting, and women [write] of their concerns with family and relational values. . . . Although many women, along with the men, wrote of the splendors of the landscape and the rigors of the road . . . there are . . . distinctions so profound as to raise the question whether women did not ultimately perceive the westward trek differently. . . . The diaries of women differ from the accounts of the men in both simple and in subtle ways. In the diaries of the women for example, the Indians are described as helpful guides and purveyors of services far more often than they are described as enemies. Although the women universally feared the Indians, they nevertheless tell, with some amusement, that their farmer husbands were not always good buffalo hunters, coming back to the wagon parties empty-handed and later trading shirts with the Indians for salmon and dried buffalo meat. The women, in the naturalness of their telling, offer a new perception of the relations between the emigrants and the Indians. Having no special stake in asserting their bravery, having no special need to affirm their prowess, the women correct the historical record as they write of the daily exchanges by which the Indians were part of life of the road.

forests and their wonderful vividness, green on all the near approaches and changing with wonderful blend from green to [ethereal] blue, and on the distant margin rested the shade of blue, so intense, so indescribably beautiful that no power of words can express the wonderful panorama of beauty with which my soul was entranced. Seated on eternal snow, looking from over these mountains and hills, across wide valleys into dark glens, above the roar of wind or of water, I was lost in infinity.[48]

Chapter 4: Native American Women

When thousands of white settlers flooded onto the American frontier in the 1800s, they moved onto lands that were not empty, but were inhabited by millions of Native Americans. The impact of the settlers was immediate—and often extremely destructive. The white settlers introduced diseases such as smallpox, measles, and scarlet fever, which were deadly to the Native Americans because they had no natural immunity to them; as many as two out of three people were killed in some tribes. Weakened by such epidemics, Native Americans often had a difficult time resisting the influx of settlers to the frontier.

Perhaps the most fundamental disruption was the clash of cultures, as many white Americans refused to accept Native American society as one profoundly different from their own. Unlike the settlers, who valued rugged individualism, Native Americans placed the needs of the community before individual desires. In this system, according to Theda Perdue in *Sifters: Native American Women's Lives*, Native Americans "lived in large, extended households where women worked together, delivered and cared for each other's children, shared rituals and celebrations, and socialized and trained the next generation."[49]

In their communal lives, Native American women played very different roles in society than white women did. While pioneer women were expected to be subservient to men and were not allowed to vote, much less participate in government, many native females had political power and authority over the decisions of their tribes. For example, women were consulted before a tribe went to war, before it made peace, and in many other areas of concern.

Roles in Daily Life

While native women sometimes shared power with men, each gender had its own specific roles to play in daily life. As Carolyn Niethammer writes in *Daughters of the Earth:* "Men and women worked in partnership to most effectively exploit their environment—there were men's tasks and there were women's tasks, and both were valued and necessary for survival."[50]

The roles women played in many Native American societies were dictated by age. Among the Pawnee who lived on the Great Plains along the Oregon Trail, the oldest women of the household cared for the small children and were referred to as "grandmother"—no matter what their actual biological relation to the children. Small children were fed by their grandmothers at mealtimes and sometimes shared beds with them at night. Grandmothers also directed younger women as they performed the cooking and cleaning chores.

Older women, those between the ages of forty and sixty, were the most respected women in Apache society in Arizona. These women were selected as female chiefs who oversaw tribal decisions that concerned women's duties. They organized trips to hunt for medicinal herbs and supervised meals for celebrations and ceremonies. Using rituals and knowledge of the environment to predict the weather, female chiefs determined what quantities of certain supplies, such as corn, would be stored before each winter. Chiefs also advised young mothers on childcare and oversaw those religious rituals and ceremonies that were performed exclusively by women.

In turn, women of the tribe paid their respects to female chiefs by giving them generous gifts. Part of this wealth was redistributed to the poor, the sick, and the elderly. With all these responsibilities, a female chief filled many roles. As Niethammer writes: "To fill her moccasins today would require a social worker, a family counselor, a pediatrician, a home extension agent, a business adviser, a minister's wife, a volunteer, and a favorite aunt."[51]

Providing Shelter

The Apache were nomadic people who made annual journeys to the Great Plains to hunt buffalo. There they met with other tribes such as the Cheyenne, the Crow, and the Blackfoot. All these tribes lived in portable cone-shaped tents called tepees. It was the sole responsibility of women to construct these shelters, to repair them, and to erect them at campsites.

To build a tepee, women first had to undertake the laborious task of curing twelve to fourteen buffalo skins, stretching, scraping, and tanning them. The final step was to dry the skins in the sun, a process that also bleached them to pure white. Once the hides were ready, a woman enlisted female friends and relatives for several days of labor to stitch the hides together. The women did this with delicate buffalo bone needles and thread that was made from tightly rolled sinew taken from the buffalo.

Cooking for Fifty People

The Pawnee lived on the vast grasslands in present-day Nebraska. The Oregon Trail passed directly through their ancestral lands. Until they were forced onto reservations in 1860, the Pawnee lived in large earth lodges that housed as many as eight families—up to fifty men, women, and children in each one. Much of the work inside the lodge was performed by women, as Gene Weltfish explains in *The Lost Universe:*

> There were two main meals a day . . . both serving all. In operation this meant that the woman who cooked the meal had raised all the vegetables in her own gardens, had dried and preserved them and kept them in her storage pit, and that all the meat she served was dried and packed by her on the buffalo hunt, carried back to the village (on her back or by the dogs she raised). . . . [Before settlers brought trade goods], the clay pot she cooked in would have been made by her . . . and she [made] the large buffalo-horn ladle with which she served, the wooden mortar and pestle in which the mush was pounded, and . . . the wooden bowls and buffalo-horn spoons in which the food was served, the rush mats on which the people sat, and all the clothing they wore. Every day, morning or evening, she would serve twenty, thirty, forty, or fifty people a meal.

When the cover was finished, it was put on a frame with the vent closed, and a fire was built inside. This smoking process softened the hide and cured it, leaving it a cream color. When the work was done, a feast was held to honor the women who made the tepee. Prayers were offered to ensure happiness, success, safety, and long life to the tepee's owners.

The tepees of the plains peoples were some of the most clever shelters ever invented. They were lightweight and could be set up in a few minutes. The translucent skin allowed light in during the day yet kept out wind, rain, ice, and snow. Working with only buffalo skin and wooden poles, the women of the plains provided shelter for their families in an often harsh and inhospitable climate.

Women as Traders

Women also used buffalo skins to make long robes that kept their families warm during frigid winters. It took weeks of skillful labor to make a single robe. When thousands of settlers began streaming onto the Great Plains, buffalo robes were highly desirable trade goods, so by producing these robes, women took on the role of providers for their entire tribes. For example, in the 1840s, one French trader bought thousands of buffalo robes all of them obtained and tanned by Native American women. In return, Native Americans received wool blankets, bolts of bright cloth, cheap guns, butcher knives, and beads. While men took the guns, women used the cloth and beads to make their families' clothing. They also used the butcher knives to skin and butcher still more buffalo.

In later years, men were sometimes eliminated from the trading equation altogether as female settlers bartered directly with Indian women. As Glenda Riley writes in *Women and Indians on the Frontier, 1825–1915:*

> Both on the trail and in their new homes, [white] women began to barter needles and thread, processed foods such as flour, articles of apparel, and trifles with natives, who usually offered fresh foods in return. Women's accounts frequently mentioned [Native] American . . . women bringing to them butter, eggs, potatoes, corn, pumpkins, melons, strawberries, blackberries, venison and other fresh meats, fish, and dried salmon. . . . Many women also became interested in obtaining specialized Indian products and crafts for themselves. They grew skillful at bargaining for buffalo hides and robes, antelope and elk clothing, moccasins, baskets, and beadwork. . . . Buffalo robes were . . . coveted, so much so that at least one woman agreed to surrender her shawl to obtain one.[52]

Skilled Artisans

In the southwest regions of present-day New Mexico, Arizona, and southern Colorado, Native American women took on the roles of basket makers, blanket weavers, and potters. These items were as valued by settlers as buffalo robes on the plains.

Baskets served both ceremonial and practical functions and were basic necessities for Native American women. In daily life, baskets were used as trays, bowls, jars, hats, hampers, and backpacks. Tightly woven baskets coated with pine sap on the inside were even used to hold water. Decorations ranged from geometric designs to star and flower themes and animal representations.

Weaving a Navajo blanket or rug was difficult and time-consuming work. It has been estimated that the production of a three-by-five-foot rug took a

The Native American tribes of the Great Plains were nomadic people who lived in portable tepees like these. It was the responsibility of the tribes' women to build and maintain the tepees.

woman four hundred hours—from shearing the sheep to spinning the yarn to working on the loom.

Pottery making is another ancient art, known to the New Mexico Pueblo tribes for thousand of years. Pueblo potters were women, and the art was learned at an early age, with young girls sitting beside their mothers and working small bits of clay. Because some of the vessels were used in religious rituals, gathering the clay for pottery was considered a sacred act, to be performed by women in absolute silence. After gathering 150 pounds of clay in a blanket, and positioning the burden on her back, each woman tied the blanket ends around her forehead and made the long journey back to the pueblo to make pottery. The designs on the pottery were geometrical representations of mountains, clouds, and rainbows. Plants and animals were also painted, including the sunflower, the cotton plant, the parrot, and the turkey.

Pueblo women in New Mexico make pottery vessels. Pueblo potters were typically female, and their craft was passed down from generation to generation.

These items were in great demand by travelers and settlers, especially after the Santa Fe Railroad started bringing thousands of visitors to the Southwest frontier in the 1880s. Some women were able to take advantage of this situation, supporting their families through sales of innovative and inspirational pottery.

Working for Settlers

Many other Native American women filled less-rewarding roles than weaver or potter. They worked at a variety of jobs including washing dishes and clothes and cleaning homes. These women were usually paid for their work in foods such as salt, sugar, and bread.

The most common role played by Native American women in settlers' homes was that of nursemaid. Many of these women performed admirably in this role, despite the common stereotype of the era that Indians would kidnap or kill white children if given a chance. Such misconceptions were addressed in a letter written by army wife Eveline

Alexander about a teenage Apache girl hired to take care of her newborn baby. Writing to her father in New York, Alexander stated:

> I wish the grandmothers of the young one, who are so afraid of her "falling" into the hands of the Apachees could have looked in upon us a while ago. They would have seen the infant prodigy awake in her cradle, cooing to herself, and being rocked to sleep by a bona fide wild Apachee, who a week ago was roaming the mountains [naked]. . . . [The Apache nurse seems] to love to be with the baby [and] is quite useful already in drawing around its wagon and rocking the cradle.[53]

While working as nurses, some Native American women also acted as cultural ambassadors, teaching white children Indian languages, customs, foods, and games. Women sang traditional songs to their charges, showed them dances, and made them clothing that featured beautiful beadwork.

Preparing for Battle

While some Native American teenagers worked for white families, there were ongoing violent conflicts between the tribes and the U.S. military in many areas. And with war an inherent part of the culture for many tribes, Native American men and women were occupied with war on a nearly constant basis. As with most other cultures under siege, both genders supported military operations. As Carolyn Niethammer writes:

> [Women] could not help but be involved in martial activities. Most Indian women limited their participation to helping outfit their brothers and husbands for their expeditions, but other, stronger willed and more individualistic women became warriors in their own right. . . .
>
> When a war party was getting ready to go out on a raid, the camp or village was always full of activity. Women were hurrying to complete extra pairs of moccasins for the men and getting together foods that could be packed and taken along. Women who had lost sons and husbands or other relatives in previous battles were apt to visit the lodge of a distinguished warrior and urge him to wipe away their tears with enemy blood.[54]

Women also took on spiritual roles, performing rituals and ceremonies meant to bring luck and safety to the men. On the southern Great Plains, before Comanche warriors went on a raid, the young women of the tribe sang battle songs that recounted legendary victories of the past. At Apache camps, women performed sacred dances before the departure of a war party. In the Dakota Territory girls and young women of the Mandan tribe fasted while the men were off in battle, returning to holy sites each day to pray and make offerings to the gods for the safe return of their men.

Peacemakers on the Prairies

It was not uncommon for Native American women to develop close bonds with their white counterparts on the frontier. In *Women and Indians on the Frontier, 1825–1915*, Glenda Riley quotes from several women's journals that describe cordial cultural exchanges between Native American women and women settlers:

> [Visits] between white women and native women . . . fostered warm feelings. One trail woman of the 1850s who visited some Sioux women came away favorably impressed by both their hospitality and their skill with a needle. Another female migrant of the 1860s recorded frequent and very genial social calls between her friends and "the Cherokee Ladies." A Mormon woman added that the Indian women whom she visited were "really friendly." She remarked that they had enjoyed "quite a dish of conversation" together. . . .

> Pleasant contacts between white and native women often blossomed into deeper associations. Once army wife Alice Baldwin had invested some time in crimping and waving native women's hair, she discovered that "thereafter the Indian women were my firm friends, and rendered me various favors and kindnesses." She commented perceptively that they were brought together by "feminine vanity and tastes," which she felt were "much the same the world over, no matter what the race or color." On one occasion, Baldwin consented to undress partially to allow Indian women to see the paraphernalia that she wore. "Crinoline and corsets they marveled at, but did not admire," she remarked. As they examined her various articles of clothing and fussed over her beautifully dressed hair . . . [Baldwin] wrote that as she sat among them, "listening to their chatter and laughter, and no doubt passing uncomplimentary comments about me, I felt that it all meant sincerity, which does not always prevail in a cultured and fashionable society."

Scalp Dancers and Prisoners

Even during times of war, life in a Native American village retained a sense of normalcy as women gardened, made clothes, prepared food, and took care of children. When a successful war party returned with many bloody scalps, however, women led frenzied celebrations that combined joyousness and revenge. These widespread practices entailed hanging the scalps atop long poles and waving them around like flags. Accompanied by fast-paced ceremonial songs and whirling dances, women achieved a state of furious excitement bordering on hysteria. Niethammer explains the motivation for these celebrations:

> They had been conditioned to the war psychology since they were children, just as the men had been, and they took part in the prewar rituals, working themselves into a high state of anger and resentfulness. It was they who felt the economic loss when a brother or husband was killed, and they who were condemned to years of widowhood when their men were killed. It is no wonder they were angry at the enemy. Yet most women were denied the excitement or the release that the men found in combat. The women had to wait until the men returned from battle with scalps . . . for the victory celebration was the proper time and place for the average Indian woman to release her tensions.[55]

While some women celebrated victory, others were destined to assume the role of prisoner of war—at least in conflicts between Native American tribes. Traditionally, when an enemy raided a village, men were killed but women and children were spared. Among the Gros Ventre on the Montana frontier, captive girls and young women were given to families who had lost relatives in previous battles. When the Ogalala of the northern plains captured women, the prisoners were given the option of marrying their captors or returning to their tribes. Among the Yuma in southeastern Arizona, women prisoners were forced to participate in the victory dance but after the celebrations were over, the women were given to old men who were too frail to care for themselves. In such situations, many captive women simply assumed the roles of typical Yuma wives.

Leaders in War

In some Native American tribes, women played active roles in making war. This was the case among the Apache, who lived in the Southwest. In the 1860s, as American settlers flooded into the Southwest, Apache warriors attacked the newcomers. When soldiers were sent to protect

When Native American warriors returned with the scalps of enemies, the women of the tribe led victory celebrations that involved dancing around poles from which the scalps were hung.

the settlements, they often engaged the Native Americans in bloody battles with many casualties on both sides. Apache women aided in these battles by fulfilling time-honored roles within their tribes. Women called for the formation of war parties, prepared food for warriors, and dressed the injuries of the wounded. One Apache woman named Lozen, however, took on the nontraditional roles of shaman and female warrior.

Lozen was the younger sister of the famous Apache warrior Victorio. She dressed like a man and fought like a man. She took part in warrior ceremonies, sang war songs, and directed the dances of the war parties before going into battle. Lozen was also credited with possessing the psychic powers of a shaman, which allowed her to "see" the enemy and predict their movements. To do so, she recited a chant and turned slowly in a circle. The direction of the enemy was determined when her palms began to tingle. If the enemy was very close, her palms were said to turn purple.

Lozen had other remarkable survival skills as well. When in need of food out on the trail, she could single-handedly kill and butcher longhorn cattle with her knife. According to Apache warrior

Kaywaykla, this was "a feat that few men would undertake."[56] Although Lozen was unusual in Apache culture, she was respected, as Laura Jane Moore writes in an essay in *Sifters: Native American Women's Lives:*

> Lozen forswore [Apache] gender norms. But although she did not marry, did not have children, did not perform women's typical tasks and instead excelled at masculine pursuits, her community perceived her as neither a threat nor a deviant. Quite the contrary, it celebrated her powerful cross-gender position. Women warriors may have been unusual in Apache history, but they were also admired, even revered, and Lozen remains emblematic of that tradition. Almost invisible to the American authorities, her reputation and daring exploits survived in [Apache legends].[57]

Working for Peace

Not all women were supportive of war, and some took on the roles of peacekeepers. For example, Olive Oatman described

the attitude of Mohave women in the Arizona Territory while the men were preparing for war: "Those of them who had husbands and brothers enlisted in the expedition tried every expedient in their power to dissuade them from it. They accused them of folly and a mere lust for war and prayed them not thus to expose their own lives and the lives of dependent ones."[58]

While the Mohave women tried to prevent war, Thoc-me-tony, or Sarah Winnemucca, used her language skills to ensure the ultimate survival of her tribe. Winnemucca was a member of the Paiute tribe, born in 1844 at Humboldt Sink in what is now northern Nevada. When she was only sixteen years old she took on the role of mediator and interpreter at Camp McDermitt in northeastern Nevada, helping to mediate a peace treaty between the Paiute and the U.S. government. As part of the agreement, the Paiute agreed to move to the Pyramid Lake Reservation in southeastern Oregon in exchange for annual supplies such as clothes, dry goods, and farm implements.

The government, however, never delivered the promised materials. Winnemucca, stung by the injustice, traveled to San Francisco in 1879 to give lectures on the poor treatment her tribe had received from the government. Her statements on the plight of her people attracted the attention of President Rutherford B. Hayes, who promised her that the Paiute would receive a large allotment of land. The pledge, however, was never kept. In the 1880s Winnemucca left the frontier to give lectures on the East Coast. At that time she became an author and published a book about the Paiute and their treatment by the federal government.

Using her fame, Winnemucca secured thousands of signatures on a petition calling for the promised allotment of reservation lands to individual Paiute. Congress passed a bill to that end in 1884, but once again promises came to nothing. From 1883 to 1886, Winnemucca was a teacher, passing on Indian traditions and history to her students at a Paiute school near Lovelock, Nevada.

Although Winnemucca and others assumed nontraditional roles, the survival of Native American culture generally depended on most women performing tasks common to their gender. Although this was the focus of their society, ironically, women were not prevented from utilizing whatever skills they could develop. This freedom allowed Native American women to be leaders in war, peace, and daily life in their villages.

Chapter 5: Women in Mining Camps and Towns

The California frontier was transformed nearly overnight when gold was discovered by James Marshall at Sutter's Mill near Sacramento in January 1848. In the years following that momentous discovery, hundreds of thousands of people from nearly every country on earth and every state in the Union flooded into the region to search for gold.

The California gold rush was dominated by men; at least 90 percent of those arriving between 1849 and 1855 were male. In the boomtown of San Francisco, where the population grew from 450 in 1847 to 50,000 in 1849, 98 percent of the residents were men. While a few women lived in larger cities such as Sacramento and Stockton, many of the hundreds of mining towns scattered throughout the region were completely devoid of women. In 1853 Abby Mansur described the situation in a town called Horse Shoe Bar, in California:

> I tell you the [women] are in great demand in this country no matter whether they are married or not . . . it is all the go here for Ladys to leave [their] Husbands, two out of three do it. There is a first rate Chance for a single woman, she can have her choice of thousands. [I] wish mother was here, she could marry a rich man and not have to lift her hand to do her work.[59]

This shortage of females provided golden opportunities for those few who made the arduous journey to California. Gold rush women were able to defy nineteenth-century conventions and become successful entrepreneurs, opening restaurants, boardinghouses, and saloons. Some followed more traditional roles, acting as teachers, laundresses, farm wives, seamstresses, and cooks, while others performed "men's work," as miners, physicians, stagecoach drivers, and mule tenders. One enterprising Spanish woman even entertained miners as a bullfighter. Many others used their talents to entertain men by singing and dancing. And, as with most boomtowns, women also worked as prostitutes and as managers of brothels.

Whatever the role, many gold rush women made more money than the miners who labored from sunup to sundown. Their wages also far exceeded those of working women back East at a time when females were only hired to perform the most menial labor. As an unsigned letter from California in 1850 states: "A smart woman can do very well in this country—true there are not

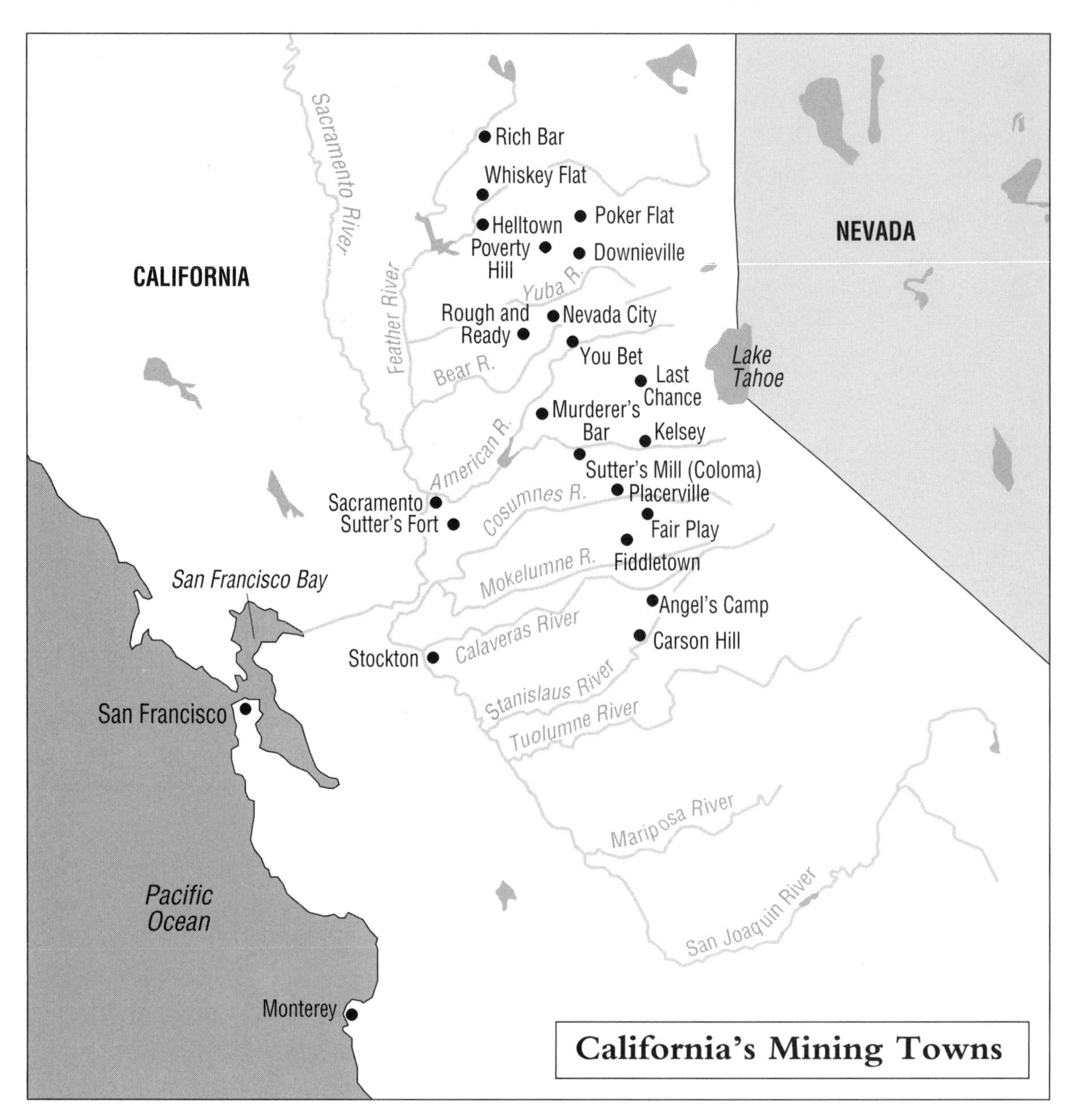

California's Mining Towns

many comforts and one must work all the time and work hard but [there] is plenty to do and good pay. . . . It is the only country that I was ever in where a woman received anything like a just compensation for her work."[60]

Cooking for the Crowds

Some women were able to utilize their cooking skills to great advantage. In fact, as men across the country joined the gold rush, it was said that if a woman could cook at all she could make good money in California. In 1850 pioneer Margaret Frink described one woman crossing the desert who had obviously taken that statement to heart. Frink recalled that "a negro woman came tramping along through the heat and dust, carrying a cast-iron baking oven on her head, with her provisions and blanket piled on top—all she possessed in the world—bravely pushing on to California."[61]

This African American woman would probably have been denied the right to open her own business in the East during this era of legalized slavery in the South and overt racism in the North. There were no such restrictions in boomtowns, however. In Sonora, a former slave known as Aunt Maria made over one hundred dollars a week cooking for a local family. She used the funds to open her own boardinghouse and earned a reputation as an excellent cook who could be called upon to cater weddings and banquets.

While Aunt Maria prepared many types of food, some women made fortunes specializing in a single product. For example, pies filled with meat or fruit such as dried apples were popular among miners because they could be purchased for consumption before, during, or after work. A skilled cook could make such pies with little equipment and little investment other than hard work, as one anonymous California woman wrote in 1852:

> I have made about $18,000 worth of pies—about one third of this has been clear profit. One year I dragged my own wood off the mountains and chopped it, and I have never had [anyone to help] me in this country. . . . I baked [$11,000 worth of pies] in one little iron skillet, a considerable portion by a campfire. . . . I bake about 1,200 pies per month and clear $200.[62]

Women Innkeepers

Many who were successful cooks used their profits to open boardinghouses and hotels—establishments that were in great demand as thousands of newcomers arrived in California every day. In 1849, near Nevada City, California,

Luzena Wilson took her first step on the road to fortune by the simple act of cooking biscuits over a campfire for her husband and two young sons. As she was doing so, a scruffy miner offered her five dollars for "bread made by a woman."[63] To be offered such a sum was astonishing; at this time a skilled carpenter in the East made about five dollars a week. Wilson simply stared at the miner in shock, which caused him to double his offer. After he laid a large chunk of shiny gold in her hand, Wilson quickly realized that she could capitalize on her gender and make a fortune in the new land. That night she had a dream, in which, she later wrote, "I saw crowds of bearded miners striking gold from the earth with every blow of the pick, each one seeming to leave a share for me."[64]

The next day, Wilson stocked up on groceries and set up a rough restaurant by the side of the road. She describes the activities that followed:

> I bought two boards from a precious pile belonging to a man who was building the second wooden house in town. With my own hands I chopped stakes, drove them into the ground, and set up my table. I bought provisions at a neighboring store, and when my husband came back at night he found, mid the weird light of the pine torches, twenty miners eating at my table. Each man as he rose put a dollar in my hand and said I might count him as a permanent customer. . . . From the first day [I] was well patronized, and I shortly after took my husband into partnership.[65]

Wilson's primitive restaurant quickly grew into the El Dorado Hotel, as she used her profits to enlarge it room by room. Before long, the El Dorado was housing two hundred men, each paying twenty-five dollars per week. Wilson hired cooks and waiters, but continued to work in her spare time mending clothes for the miners. When she had about five hundred dollars stashed away, she went into the banking business, loaning money for the exorbitant rate of 10 percent interest a month. Within six months, Wilson owned buildings worth twenty thousand dollars. When a fire wiped out most of Nevada City, including her hotel, Wilson built another hotel in a nearby area that later became downtown Vacaville.

Not all hotels were as grand as the El Dorado, and women who ran less fancy establishments were often forced to work very hard for their money. One unnamed woman simply set up a boardinghouse in her log cabin, which was about fourteen feet square. She lived with her husband and children in one half of the room, while crowding ten boarders into the other. Sleep was difficult as the men were often drunk, rowdy, gambling, arguing, and fighting—when not snoring loudly throughout the night. Although she made about seventy-five dollars a week, she had to prepare thirty meals a day in a very small fireplace and with no oven.

The kitchens of some boardinghouses lacked any walls at all. In 1851 Mary Ballou worked in a primitive boardinghouse with a mud floor and a leaky canvas roof. In addition to cooking, Ballou had to feed livestock as well as keep the animals out of her kitchen and dining room, as she states in a letter to her son, written in the typically unschooled manner of the era:

"Throw It into My Lye Kettle"

Historians recognize James Marshall as the person who first discovered gold at Sutter's Mill in 1848, setting off the California gold rush. What few realize, however, is that a woman named Elizabeth Bays Wimmer scientifically proved that the metal Marshall found was indeed gold.

Wimmer, who had migrated to California with her husband and seven children in 1846, was a camp cook and laundress at Sutter's Mill. She was also a soap maker who understood that the strong lye (sodium hydroxide) used in soap could be used to bring out the shiny yellow color associated with gold. When Marshall first found the gold, he was unsure what it was. No one in his crew knew what gold looked like in its natural state. Gold coins available at that time looked much shinier and whiter than the lump Marshall found. According to *They Saw the Elephant: Women in the California Gold Rush*, Wimmer told Marshall what to do with his dull, bronze-colored rock:

> I said . . . "I will throw it into my lye kettle . . . and if it is gold, it will be gold [in color] when it comes out." I finished off my soap that day and set it off to cool, and it stayed there till next morning. At the breakfast table one of the work hands raised up his head from eating and said, "I heard something about gold being discovered, what about it?" . . . I told him it was in my soap kettle. . . . A plank was brought for me to lay my soap onto, and I cut it in chunks, but it was not to be found. At the bottom of the pot was a double handful of [ash], which I lifted in my two hands, and there was my gold as bright as could be.

Somtimes I am feeding my chickens and then again I am scareing the Hogs out of my kitchen and Driving the mules out of my Dining room. You can see by the descrption . . . that I have given you of my kitchen that anything can walk into the kitchen that choeses to walk in and there being no door to shut from the kitchen into the Dining room so you can see the Hogs and mules can walk in any time day or night if they choose to do so. somtimes I am up all times a night scaring the Hogs and mules out of the House. last night . . . a large rat came down [and] pounce down onto our bed in the night. . . . I hear the Hogs

Many women in California operated hotels and boardinghouses that accommodated the huge influx of men who came in search of gold during the California gold rush.

> in my kichen turning the Pots and kettles upside down so I must drop my pen and run and drive them out.[66]

Ballou's situation was common, and there was no end to the work of running a boardinghouse. Many women labored for months with no time off. An 1850 letter from Mary Jane Megquier lists the numerous chores performed by a woman innkeeper:

> [Every day] I get up and make the coffee, then I make the biscuit, then I fry the potatoes then broil three pounds of steak, and as much liver, while . . . setting the table, at eight the bell rings and they are eating until nine. I do not sit until they are nearly all done. . . . After breakfast I bake six loaves of bread (not very big) then four pies, or a pudding then we have lamb . . . beef, pork, baked turnips, beets, potatoes, radishes, salad, and that everlasting soup, every day, dine at two, for tea we have hash, cold meat bread and butter sauce and some kind of cake and I have cooked every mouthful that has been eaten excepting one day and a half that we were on a steamboat excursion. I make six beds every day and do the washing and ironing you must think that I am very busy and when I dance all night I am obliged to trot all day and if I had not the constitution of six horses I should [have] been dead long ago.[67]

Working as a "Mineress"

While running a boardinghouse was difficult, it could not compare to the gritty work of mining. Miners worked with heavy tools while standing hip-deep in freezing water and mud. Working day in and day out, their feet and hands became numb, swollen, smashed, and rubbed raw. Some women tried their hand at this difficult work. One woman, Louisa Clapp, took on the role of what she calls a "mineress" for just one day. In a letter home, Clapp wrote: "I am sorry I learned the trade, for I wet my feet, tore my dress, spoilt a pair of new gloves, nearly froze my fingers, got an awful headache, took cold, and lost a valuable breast-pin."[68]

While most women did not actually pan for gold, many helped their husbands with the less strenuous work, such as pouring water into simple machines called rockers that were designed to separate gold flakes from dirt. Some women even struck it rich—often a result of good luck. A woman known as Mrs. H.H. Smith found, among some river rocks, a sixty-five-pound chunk of gold

"I Walked 16 Miles to See a Woman"

There were very few women in mining camps, and some men were so desperate to simply gaze upon a woman that they were willing to expend a lot of energy to do so. In California in 1849, George W. Thissell heard that a woman, Mrs. Snow, was cooking in a place called Snow's Camp. He described his reaction in his diary, reprinted in *Fools of '49*, by Laurence I. Seidman:

> Next morning I put on my best jean-pants, a pair of alligator boots, a red flannel shirt, my old wool hat lopped down over my ears. I struck out on foot to see the wonderful creature. When I arrived in Snow's Camp, it was late in the day and Mrs. Snow kept a restaurant. I ordered dinner at $1.50. While eating, I saw some eggs in a pan. On inquiry, I learned they were worth one dollar each, so I ordered one cooked. This brought my dinner to $2.50.
>
> It was dark long before I reached home, and should I live to be a hundred—I shall never forget the day I walked 16 miles to see a woman in California.

worth thirteen thousand dollars—a large fortune at that time.

In another stroke of good luck, Harriet Behrins was taking a break from her household chores when she spotted something shiny in the dirt outside her log cabin. With her cooking spoon, she pried out a large gold nugget, which she cashed in for an undisclosed sum. Another unnamed housewife did not even have to leave home to make her fortune. While sweeping the dirt floor of her log cabin she noticed glittering flakes of gold. She quickly removed the table, benches, and stove, and excavated five hundred dollars worth of gold from her kitchen floor. It turned out that, as luck would have it, her cabin had been built on a large gold seam; she hired some workers to dig, and they extracted a fortune from the floor of her humble abode.

The Entertainers

While a lucky few struck it rich, it was much more common for women to work hard in the roles of entertainers for the miners—acting, singing, dancing, and playing musical instruments for them. In return for exhibiting their talents to lonesome, homesick men, many women entertainers were well compensated. Top talent earned as much as three thousand dollars per week, and even the less gifted pulled in a thousand dollars. One particularly beautiful singer, Catherine Hayes, was able to make more than a quarter million dollars by selling seats to her performances in San Francisco at an auction. In addition, like other women who performed for miners, Hayes was showered with gold nuggets and jewelry as she performed onstage.

As word spread that professional entertainers could profit handsomely, even well-known personalities made the arduous journey to California. Perhaps the most famous entertainer to appear in San Francisco was Lola Montez, an international star at the time.

Montez was known for her signature dance known as the tarantella. When she performed the dance in San Francisco, miners whistled, stomped their feet, and howled with delight as Montez pretended that spiders were crawling all over her body. She writhed, kicked, and dug her hands into her already revealing outfit in search of attacking arachnids. A humorous review in an unnamed newspaper described the event:

> [The] Spider Dance was to represent a girl that commences dancing and finds a spider on her clothes and jumps about to shake it off. If that's it . . . then in the first part of the dance I guess she must see the spider up on the ceiling, and that it's in trying to kick the cobwebs down that she gets the spider upon her clothes. She kicked up and she kicked

Dancer Lola Montez was a popular attraction for miners in San Francisco during the gold rush.

> around in all directions, and first it was this leg and then it was the other and her petticoats were precious short. . . . The kicking match between Lola and the spiders caused this bashful observer to put his hat over his eyes and just peep over the brim. . . . If the Countess wasn't crazy, I don't know what on earth was the matter with her. She seemed to get so excited like, that she forgot that there was any man at all about there. . . . At that point the audience began stamping on the floor and the shy observer ran out of the theater, frightened that the house would come down, or she'd take her dress right off, and I couldn't stand it.[69]

Plays and theater were only part of the San Francisco entertainment scene. Some survived by playing rough saloons called "hells," where female musicians cheered up homesick male visitors by playing folk music from faraway countries. For example, a woman billed as the "Swiss Organ-girl" made several hundred dollars a month playing traditional Swiss music, while a Frenchwoman played classical music on her violin, earning about two ounces of gold dust—thirty-two dollars—a day. Such entertainment could be found in almost any of the hundreds of saloons, gambling halls, and hotel restaurants that were opened in San Francisco in the 1850s. Wherever there was dancing, singing, or acting, women entertainers provided some respite from homesickness for the hardworking miners.

"Fancy Ladies"

As was often the case wherever large numbers of men and few women congregated, some of the women who followed the gold rush worked as prostitutes. Some women from South America and China were unwittingly forced into prostitution when they signed up to work as servants in exchange for a ticket to California. Others came willingly to work in brothels, which were legally allowed to operate in the state. Whatever the background of the women, prostitution was a booming business, as Cathy Luchetti and Carol Olwell write in *Women of the West:*

> [Prostitution] existed as an art, a social service, and a thriving industry in nearly every major city. . . . It contributed substantially to local revenues, as madams in many cities were obliged to share a portion of each night's take with the local police. It began in earnest in the West during the Gold Rush, when claim-happy prospectors poured into California with high hopes of getting rich. These men had nothing more

> than the memory of feminine companionship to warm them at night, and were soon joined by the fancy ladies who came by wagon and muleback, by overland coach . . . and by ship. . . . [Prostitutes] set up shop in canvas tents or in saloon backrooms, and before long . . . the mining camps rang with laughter and drunken revelry. . . . [The] miners . . . were dazzled by the exotic plumed costumes and elaborate coiffures of the whores. With them they found elegance, companionship, sympathy, and sex—and they often treated the lowliest saloon girls with affection and respect.[70]

Prostitutes worked in mining towns with colorful names such as Bedbug, Git Up and Git, Hangtown, Hell's Delight, Chucklehead Diggings, Squabbletown, Humbug, You Bet, Poker Flats, Poverty Flat, Gouge Eye, and Whiskeytown. It is not surprising, then, that the prostitutes also picked up catchy names. According to Ron Lackmann in *Women of the Western Frontier in Fact, Fiction and Film*, miners might visit women named Contrary Mary, Spanish Queen, Little Gold Dollar, Em Straight Edge, Peg Leg Annie, and Molly b'Damned.

While the activities of the whores were roundly condemned by "respectable," or "polite," society, ironically, they were inadvertently responsible for many civic improvements. Politicians not only patronized the prostitutes, but they taxed them heavily. The moneys collected often paid for road improvements, schools, government facilities, and even the salaries of the politicians themselves. With the taxes they paid flowing into city coffers, prostitutes were generally tolerated by local authorities.

The women who ran the whorehouses—known as madams—were among the richest people in California. For example, at a time when a lucky miner might make about twenty-eight hundred dollars a year, madam Belle Cora was able to make one hundred thousand dollars. She ran Placerville's premier business, a whorehouse where dozens of women from Hawaii plied their trade.

While miners might have put what they referred to as "fancy ladies" on a pedestal, still prostitution was a dirty, dangerous, and unhealthy way for a woman to make a living. Prostitutes often began plying their trade in their early teens. Those who made it to age thirty often suffered from venereal diseases, unwanted pregnancies, alcoholism, and drug addiction. Drunken, pistol-packing customers might abuse, or even kill, prostitutes, usually without having to answer for their crime. Never accepted by polite society, prostitutes were

Women as Peacemakers

While San Francisco had five hundred saloons and forty-six gambling houses by the end of 1849, there were no police stations. Mining camps were similarly lawless. Violence and crime were rampant, and in some cases it was only the pleading of women that prevented senseless murders. In an 1852 letter, printed in *Let Them Speak for Themselves: Women in the American West, 1849–1900*, Mary Ballou describes how she prevented one killing:

> On the 9 of September there was a little fight took place in the store. I saw them strike each other through the window in the store. one went and got a pistol and started towards the other man. I never go into the store but your mothers tender heart could not stand that so I ran into the store and Beged and plead with [the man] not to kill [the other] for eight or ten minutes not to take his Life for the sake of his wife and three little children to spare his life and then I ran through the Dining room into my sleeping room and Buried my Face in my bed so as not to hear the sound of the pistol and wept Biterly. Oh I thought if I had wings how quick I would fly to the [East]. that night at the supper table [the aggressor] told the Boarders if it had not been for what [I] said to him [that guy] would have been a dead man. after he got his pashion over he said that he was glad that he did not kill him so you see that your mother has saved one Human beings Life. You see that I am tying to relieve all the suffering and trying to do all the good that I can.

mostly shunned by the very people who used their services.

By the 1860s, the colorful gold rush era was over in California. But the hardworking women who labored in restaurants, hotels, mining camps, and elsewhere helped the state become one of the most powerful in the Union. And along the way, these founding mothers of California helped define new roles for women in American society.

Chapter 6: Ranchers and Cowgirls

By the mid-1860s the best lands had been taken along the West Coast, and the new American frontier had shifted to Texas, Oklahoma, and the eastern parts of Wyoming, Colorado, and New Mexico. In this hot, dry territory, a nutritious forage called buffalo grass grew as high as a bull's horns. This grass fed hundreds of thousands of wild cows that had been roaming the plains since Spanish explorers brought cattle to the region in the eighteenth century.

After the Civil War ended in 1865, thousands of men—and a few women—saw an opportunity to make a living providing cattle for beef-hungry easterners. They rounded up cattle and then fed them on ranches on the open plains and drove them up a dusty path known as the Chisholm Trail, which linked the ranches of Texas to Abilene, Kansas. From there, the Atchison, Topeka and Santa Fe Railroad transported the fattened animals to slaughterhouses in Chicago.

These ranchers, cowboys, and cowgirls were often poorly paid laborers who rode endless miles in scorching sun, snow, wind, and rain. Few made fortunes—the western livestock industry was controlled by a handful of men who owned more than half of the West's 23 million cows.

Despite the harsh realities, the fifteen years between 1865 and 1880 were widely known as the golden age of the cowboy. The lonesome cowpoke, riding his pony, dressed in Levi jeans, Stetson hat, and cowboy boots, fired the public imagination. This icon came to represent the frontier, freedom, and the American ideal. This image, however, was decidedly not applied to women. As Elizabeth Clair Flood writes in *Cowgirls: Women of the Wild West:*

> In the nineteenth century, a woman's place was in the home, not out on the range herding cattle, branding calves, or breaking horses: [Nineteenth-century] society considered this behavior unladylike. . . . Living on the fringes of society to run a cattle ranch was a preposterous vocation for a woman and represented uncharted territory.[71]

Ranch Women

While polite society might have shunned the idea of a woman working on a ranch, most ranches were family businesses where men, women, and children worked together. Yet ranching was a grubby affair, and most ranches offered little in the way of luxury. Some families lived in covered wagons, Indian-style tepees, or little lean-tos built into hillsides. Spiders, rats, snakes, fleas, and scorpions lurked in the dust. At night, ranchers slept on mattresses made from old feed bags stuffed with hay, also known as "Montana feathers."

Small ranches might have twenty or thirty cattle. Days were filled with work and nights were lonely. Cattleman Charles Goodnight's wife, Mary Ann, once said she adopted three chickens as if they were friends: "They were something I could talk to."[72]

The loneliness experienced by Goodnight's wife was an occupational

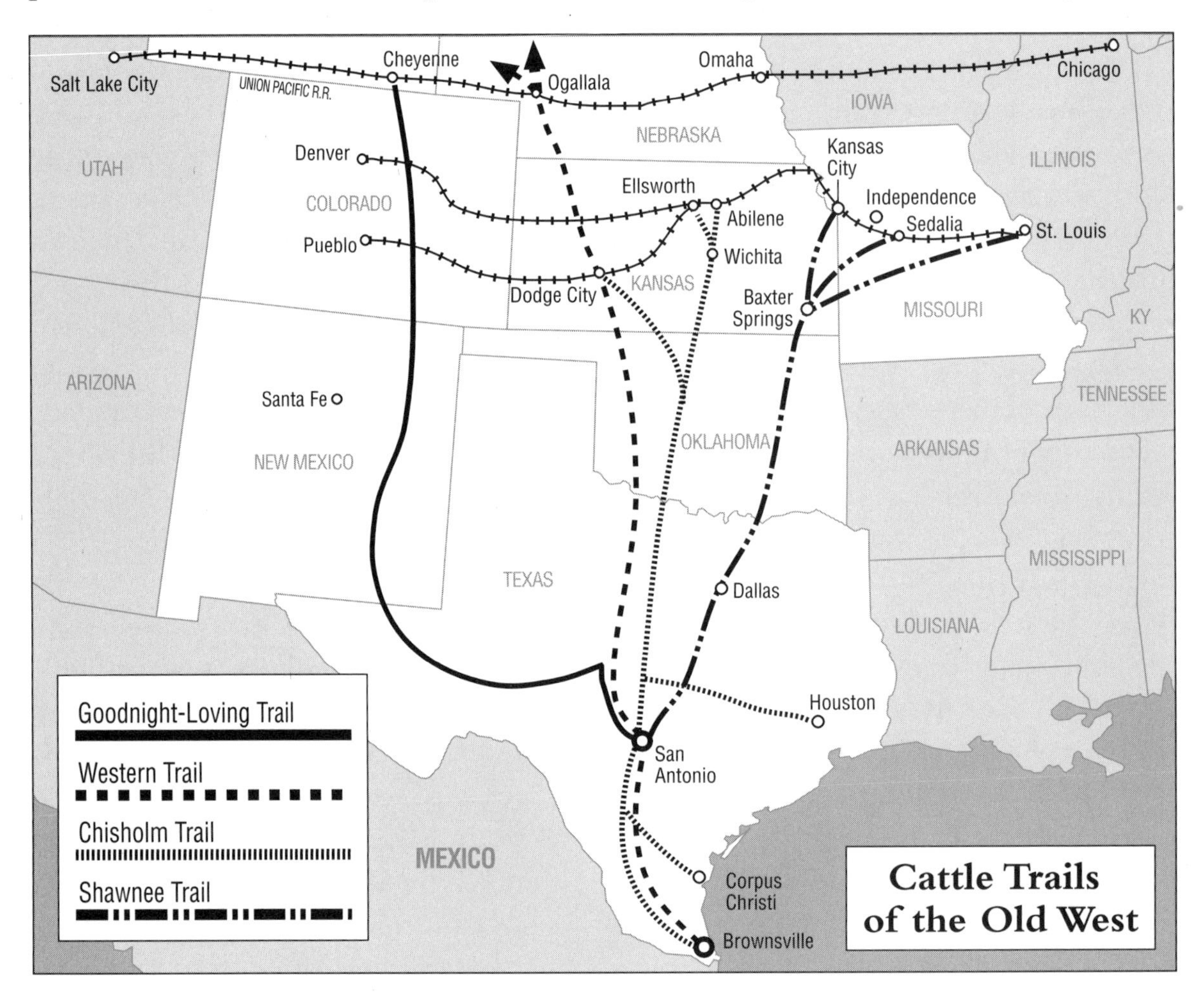

hazard of ranch families. Not only were ranches isolated, but annual cattle drives meant that husbands were forced to leave wives for months at a time as they hit the Chisholm Trail to herd their cows to rail lines hundreds of miles away. During these periods, wives were left alone to take care of all other ranch business—and their children. One unnamed ranch wife described her situation: "I know I have baked a thousand biscuits for his trips. . . . The time he spent on the trail seemed very long to me, as I stayed home, took care of the babies and the place."[73]

In such situations women entertained themselves by improving their living situations. For example, Ella Dumont, a skilled artisan, used her time to make furniture. In *Texas Tears and Texas Sunshine*, she describes her first project, and the reaction of her male neighbors:

> We had been eating on two large benches, and I made my mind up that I would make a table. There were plenty of tools—saws, hammers, etc. The baby was asleep, so I went to work, and had good luck with it. Everything measured out, and by the middle of the afternoon I had a first class table . . . with a large drawer for cold victuals. For knobs on the drawer I sawed a large spool in two and attached them with two horseshoe nails in each. . . . I was rather proud of the job if I did do it myself. . . . That afternoon when the men came in, Mr. Sullivan was the first. He asked who had been there. I said, "No one at all." He asked, "Where did the table come from?" "I made it," I said. He laughed rather incredulously; he thought I was joking. I could hardly convince him I really did. He examined the drawer and everything and said it beat anything he had ever seen made by a woman. He went out and brought in Mr. Savage to look at it. He would hardly believe either at first. He said there was not a man in the country that could do half as good a job. They gave me such a "blow-up" I got rather plagued out and almost wished I had not made it.[74]

While a few made furniture, it was more common for ranch wives to raise chickens, hunt for wild turkeys and deer, and harvest and preserve wild fruit such as plums, grapes, and berries. Dumont made extra money with her sewing machine, sewing buckskin pants, vests, and gloves for cowboys.

Cattle Queens

While women like Dumont played important roles as ranch wives, even in the earliest frontier times, there were women who took ranching matters into their own hands and became known as cattle queens. One of the first was Doña Maria del Carmen Cavillo, who inherited her father's ranch in 1814. According to Candace Savage in *Cowgirls*, "She is said to have cut a fine figure as she flew across her lands on her white stallion, issuing instructions to her crew of cowhands. A superb rider and markswoman, she was noted (and tut-tutted) for her flowing black hair, her scandalous male attire and her financial success."[75]

There were many more women ranchers to follow. By the middle of the nineteenth century, women made up almost 47 percent of the white population of Texas, where a large majority of state residents were ranchers. One of the most famous cattle queens was Elizabeth Johnson Williams, a Missouri-born woman who arrived in Hays County, Texas, in 1852.

Williams took on many roles on her way to earning a fortune in the cattle business. She began working as a bookkeeper for cattlemen in Austin when she was eighteen years old. Unhappy with her wages, Williams became an author, writing western stories such as *The Haunted House Among the Mountains* and *The Passion Flower* for national magazines. She parlayed the money she earned from writing into a small fortune by taking on the role of investor. After studying the market, she doubled her money by investing in a Chicago cattle company. In 1871 Williams officially registered her "CY" brand with the state of Texas. Two days later she began buying land and cattle in Travis County, paying for her first ten acres with three thousand gold dollar coins.

Williams quickly became a living legend as a Texas cattle queen when she became the first women to ride the Chisholm Trail with cattle marked by her own brand. On these runs, Williams drove a buggy while cowboys rode herd on her cattle.

In 1879, at age thirty-six, Williams married but did not turn her business over to her husband. Instead, she shocked the public when she defied tradition and drew up a premarital contract that allowed her to retain control of her financial affairs and keep her property separate from her husband's. After the cattle queen's death in 1924, friends found a fortune in money and jewelry stashed in hiding places throughout her ranch.

Cowgirls and Female Cowboys

The well-publicized success of Elizabeth Johnson Williams helped to entice other women into the cattle business. While few achieved the wealth or fame that Williams did, several surpassed her feats of daring. For example, Mary Ann Goodnight drove a supply wagon and was crew boss of cowhands on one cattle drive. Cornelia Adair, an Englishwoman, rode an incredible four hundred miles on one arduous drive.

Some women possessed special skills as horsewomen that proved them superior to men. When Mary Bunton rode the Chisholm Trail in the 1880s, she was the only person able to handle a particularly contrary Spanish pony. She described her experiences with the horse in a book she wrote, *A Bride on the Old Chisholm Trail in 1886*, a portion of which appears in Jo Ella Powell Exley's *Texas Tears and Texas Sunshine:*

I got the pony and he proved a joy and was the best gaited saddle pony I ever rode. However, he would never let a man ride him or even catch him if he was loose. Every cowboy in the outfit tried time and again to conquer him but they gave up in despair. Finally, I laid the law down to them, one and all, that none of them was ever to get on his back again. When they attempted to saddle him for me to ride, he would paw, kick and fight every man that came near but the minute he heard my voice, he would neigh for me and as soon as I was in the saddle he was gentle and obeyed the slightest

Although a few skilled cowgirls were able to find work as ranch hands, many others were forced to disguise themselves as men in order to be considered for ranch work.

> touch of my hand on the bridle. I had ridden him many times as much as thirty-five or forty miles on certain occasions and the going was so easy that I was not fatigued and my pony was none the worse for the trip. When I grew tired of riding horseback on the trail, he was turned in with the herd or attached to the chuck wagon.[76]

Bunton learned her equestrian skills in exclusive private schools. Other cowgirls, however, found their way into working cattle under more unusual circumstances—giving up their roles as women to spend their lives as men. Often this was the only way they could find employment. For example, Elizabeth Guerin was a widow with thirteen children. Known as Mountain Charley, she dressed like a man "as the only resort from starvation or worse." Guerin worked as a cattle driver and enjoyed her adopted male role: "I began to rather like the freedom of my new character. . . . I could go where I chose, [and] do many things which while innocent in themselves, were debarred by propriety from association with the female sex."[77]

Willie Matthews was another woman who circumvented nineteenth-century conventions by dressing in men's clothes. She got her first job in 1884 when a trail boss named Sam Dunn Houston rode into Clayton, New Mexico, hoping to hire some cowboys for a cattle drive to Colorado. There was no one available except for a youngster Houston described as "a kid of a boy"[78] named Willie. Houston hired Willie, who proved to be a very good employee. As Houston later recalled:

> [The] kid would get up [on] the darkest stormy nights and stay with the cattle until the storm was over. He was good natured, very modest, didn't use cuss words or tobacco, and [was] always pleasant. . . . I was so pleased with him that I wished many times that I could find two or three more like him.[79]

When the ride was nearly completed, Houston and the other cowboys were startled to see a well-dressed young woman approach. When she was twenty feet away she laughed and said, "Mr. Houston, you don't know me do you?" Houston replied, "Kid, is it possible that you are a lady?"[80] Houston ordered Matthews to explain her ruse. She said her father had been a trail boss who would tell her exciting stories of cattle drives when she was ten years old, and Matthews had sworn that one day she would get a job as a cowpuncher, or cowboy.

Pistol-Packing Cowgirls

Whether living on a ranch or traveling the trail on a cattle drive, women ranchers were as dependent on their weapons as men were. While ropes and whips kept cattle in line, rifles and pistols afforded women protection in a dangerous world. According to Joyce Gibson Roach in *The Cowgirls*, there was a code for pistol-packing cattlewomen that concerned the use of guns—and it was not about fair play. The women's gun code advised: "Strange men [are OK] to shoot. Shoot first, ask questions later. If you shoot a man in the back, he rarely returns fire. Scare a man to death even if you do not intend to kill him. [And] if a man needs killing, do it."[81]

The Cattle Queen of Montana

While some women became successful cattle queens, they often had to challenge tradition and long-standing rules to do so. For Libby Smith Collins, it was discriminatory railroad regulations that stood between her and a successful cattle drive.

Libby owned a ranch with her husband, Nat, in Choteau, Montana. Every year Nat drove their cattle hundreds of rough miles to the Great Falls railroad depot and accompanied the animals on the long train ride to the Chicago stockyards where he was paid for his cows. In 1886, a few days before the fall cattle drive, Nat fell ill. While a woman had never made such a drive alone, Libby was determined to go. She successfully drove her cows to Great Falls but was informed that railroad regulations prohibited a woman from traveling with stock on a cattle train, or even riding along if she paid full fare.

Libby demanded a meeting with a representative of the Chicago firm that handled her cattle. He sympathized with her plight and telegraphed railroad officials in St. Paul, Minnesota. Officials there granted Libby a special permit to ride the train. It has been said that as she boarded the train the cowboys cheered and chanted, "Success to Aunty Collins, the Cattle Queen of Montana." Upon arrival in Chicago, Libby shrewdly bargained an excellent price for her stock, several hundred dollars more than what she had previously been offered. When her story was reported in a cattleman's magazine, the newly ordained Cattle Queen of Montana became a legend. In the following years she accompanied her stock to Chicago annually, and her exploits were often reported in the press.

Women took on the roles of gunslinger for a variety of reasons. One unnamed Texas ranchwoman used her .45 caliber pistol to blow off a cowboy's head when he pinched her ankle in what she perceived as an unwanted sexual gesture. More commonly, women used their guns to punish rustlers—those who stole cattle. When five hundred head of Cassie Redwine's stock disappeared in the Texas Panhandle, she hunted for the outlaws with her ranch cowboys. The group soon found the rustlers' camp, but the outlaws were not there. Redwine hid in the bushes with the others and awaited the return of the desperadoes. As they rode into camp, Redwine used her gun to kill the group's leader known as Black Pedro. The rest were captured, given a quick trial, and shot by a firing squad. A newspaper reported, however, that "Cassie had nothing to do with that part of it."[82]

In such a lawless atmosphere, many women carried concealed weapons at all times. In Arizona, Molly Owens made a customized apron with a special pocket to hide her pistol. When a strange cowboy approached, Owens could innocently put her hand in the pocket—and keep her finger on the trigger—until she was sure of the man's intentions.

Not all women needed guns to enforce western justice, however, and some took on the roles of expert ropers. When a rancher known as Mrs. Victor Daniels noticed two cattle rustlers riding off with her herd, she grabbed her lasso and jumped onto her horse. When she caught up to the outlaws, Daniels threw her lasso around the neck of one man and jerked him off his horse. As he lay strangling on the ground, Daniels instructed the other rustler to drive her cattle back home. After this was done, the survivor left the scene while his unfortunate companion lay dead with a broken neck.

Bad Girls

The roping and shooting skills honed by some cowgirls were not always used for lawful purposes. Although it was unusual, some western women turned to crime, oftentimes learning their criminal ways from men.

In 1889 Rose Dunn took with the notorious train-robbing, cattle-rustling Doolin gang in the Oklahoma Territory. This twenty-year-old woman, known as the Rose of Cimarron, had been raised in a convent in Kansas but was an expert roper and shooter. After she fell in love with the handsome George "Bitter Creek" Newcomb, a member of the Doolin gang, she moved into the Doolin hideout. According to Joyce Gibson Roach, the Rose of Cimarron took on the roles of "nurse, scout, spy, courier, and horse holder . . . [and the] entire gang worshipped her."[83]

The Rose of Cimarron proved that she was fit for the role of outlaw when a posse caught up with the Doolins in the town of Ingalls, in the Oklahoma Territory. After a brief shootout with the men, Newcomb lay wounded in the street. Rose saw the gun battle from her second-story hotel window and sprang into action. She strapped two pistols around her waist and grabbed a rifle. She tied the bedsheets together to make a rope and lowered herself down to the street. Dodging bullets, Rose delivered the pistols to Newcomb while returning fire with her rifle. This drove away the posse and allowed the Doolin gang to escape. Newcomb soon died, however, and the widowed Rose of Cimarron gave up her outlaw ways to marry into a wealthy Oklahoma family.

Although the Rose of Cimarron was gone, the Doolin gang continued to corrupt young women. In the 1890s Annie McDoulet, seventeen years old, and Jennie Stevens, sixteen years old, took up with the gang and earned the nicknames Cattle Annie and Little Britches, respectively. These young women were horse and cattle rustlers who were always heavily armed. The women also acted as spies, keeping track of the activities of the local sheriff and other lawmen.

Despite the efforts of their young female spies, the Doolin gang was eventually arrested. Cattle Annie and Little Britches ran away to the town of Pawnee, but were followed by Marshals Bill Tilghman and Steve Burke. Roach describes the capture of these two female outlaws:

> Little Britches saw the men coming, leaped out a window [on]to a horse, and galloped off. Marshal Tilghman, not wanting to shoot a woman in spite of the fact that she had no compunction about emptying her gun on him, shot her horse instead. The horse fell on the girl, no doubt saving the marshal a foot race to capture her. She fought like a wild cat until Tilghman spanked her. . . . Meanwhile, Marshal Burke captured Cattle Annie when she leaned out a window to shoot at him. They, too, had a free-for-all but Burke managed to subdue his captive with a bear hug.[84]

Little Britches and Cattle Annie served only short prison sentences but became famous when their deeds were fictionalized in cheap novels and magazines popular at that time. They were following a path to fame paved by the most notorious lady of the era, Belle Starr.

Starr, a Texas resident, was by far the most famous "bad girl" of the frontier.

In the 1860s and 1870s she was known as the Petticoat Terror and the Bandit Queen of the West. Like other outlaw ladies, Starr's notoriety resulted from her choice of companions—the infamous Frank and Jesse James and the Younger brothers—outlaws who robbed stagecoaches and banks and killed several lawmen. While her deeds were sensationalized in magazine stories and dime novels, Starr was never convicted of any crime except the relatively minor offense of rustling cattle.

Wild West Sharpshooters

The exaggerated deeds of the cowgirls served to change attitudes about western women, even as the golden age of the cowboy was ending in the 1880s. Because of the publicity received by Belle Starr and others, the image of a wild and free frontier cowgirl was being widely embraced by the American public.

Much of this acceptance can be traced to women who took on the roles of performers in circuslike Wild West shows. These women variously performed astounding tricks on horseback, rode bucking broncos, and used their pistols and rifles with amazing accuracy.

The first person to "sell" this romanticized image of the cowgirl was William "Buffalo Bill" Cody, who began putting on all-male Wild West shows in theaters in the late 1860s. These productions would feature reenactments of Native Americans attacking Cody before he "killed" them in a barrage of gunfire and smoke. By the 1880s, Buffalo Bill's Wild West show was a national success. In 1885, however, his male sharpshooter suddenly quit. In desperation, Cody hired a petite cowgirl named Annie Oakley to take his place.

Oakley, born Phoebe Anne Moses, had begun winning professional shooting exhibitions when only fifteen years old. By the time she joined Buffalo Bill's show as a "shootist," the five-foot-tall Oakley was able to shoot a hole in a dime held by her husband, himself a sharpshooter, who took on the role of her assistant. She could also fire a bullet that flicked the ash off a cigarette held in his mouth. In one stunt, Oakley rested a rifle backward on top of her head and used a mirror to hit a target that was behind her back. In another, her husband threw several glass balls into the air. Oakley ran toward them, leaped over a table and grabbed a gun from it, and shot the glass balls to pieces before they hit the ground.

Oakley's gun skills made her a legend in her own time, and she was one of the most famous women in both the United States and Europe in the last decades of the nineteenth century. Dur-

A Rider for the Pony Express

Calamity Jane was one of the most famous cowgirls of the Wild West. She took on many roles, as a saloon keeper, a miner, a scout for the U.S. Army, and a bull whacker, or ox driver. She gained widespread fame when her life was fictionalized in cheap novels such as *Calamity Jane, Queen of the Plains* and *Calamity Jane, the Heroine of Whoop-up.* In 1876 Calamity Jane utilized her riding skills to deliver mail in South Dakota for the Pony Express. In her autobiography, *Life and Adventures of Calamity Jane*, she describes the experience:

> During the month of June [1876] I acted as a pony express rider carrying the U. S. mail between Deadwood and Custer, a distance of fifty miles, over one of the roughest trails in the Black Hills country. As many of the riders before me had been held up and robbed of their packages, mail and money that they carried, for that was the only means of getting mail and money between these points. It was considered the most dangerous route in the Hills, but as my reputation as a rider and quick shot was well known, I was molested very little, for the [outlaws] looked on me as being a good fellow, and they knew that I never missed my mark. I made the round trip every two days which was considered pretty good riding in that country. Remained around Deadwood all that summer visiting all the camps within an area of one hundred miles.

One of the Wild West's most famous cowgirls, Calamity Jane used her riding skills to deliver mail for the Pony Express..

Sharpshooter Annie Oakley spent sixteen years touring the United States and Europe with Buffalo Bill's Wild West show and became a legend in her own time.

ing her sixteen years with Buffalo Bill, she was the top box-office draw and was said to earn more than a thousand dollars a week—more than the president of the United States was paid at that time.

Trick Riders and Calf Ropers

Buffalo Bill's was only one of the approximately 120 Wild West shows that toured the United States at the end of the nineteenth century. Inspired by the success of Oakley, other shows hired women sharpshooters hoping to compete with Buffalo Bill. For example, Pawnee Bill's Historic Wild West Show hired May Lillie to perform shootist feats from her horse's back at full gallop. Although she was a Philadelphia native who had graduated from Smith College, Lillie also astounded audiences with her roping and bronco-riding skills. When asked about her line of work, Lillie stated: "Let any normally healthy woman who is strong, screw up her courage and tackle a bucking bronco, and she will find the most fascinating pastime in the field of feminine athletic endeavor. . . . She'll have more real fun than any pink tea or theater party or ballroom ever yielded."[85]

Lucille Mulhall also defied stereotypical roles and was the first woman to be called a "cowgirl." (Well-known humorist Will Rogers coined that term after seeing her perform at the St. Louis Fair. Until that time, cowgirls were called "cowboy girls.") Mulhall was an expert equestrian—she could make her horse dance, swing around in circles, play dead, take off her hat with his mouth, sit on his haunches, and walk on his knees. After seeing her dazzle audiences with her "manly" skills, an unnamed reporter was amazed that Mulhall also practiced the "feminine arts." He wrote: "Not only could she ride, rope, and shoot, but also play the piano, recite poetry, and make mayonnaise dressing."[86]

Breaking Ground, Breaking Rules

While Lucille Mulhall and Annie Oakley were heroines to some, most cowgirls and cattle queens lived quiet lives filled with long days of labor. They worked in the cattle business, taking on roles as hired hands, cattle buyers, horse trainers, veterinarians, and other occupations. When they first started working on the frontier, these women were breaking new ground and breaking society's rules. These trendsetters changed the meaning of feminine roles while challenging themselves to achieve success in a man's world.

Chapter 7: Women in Frontier Towns

In the early years of the nineteenth century, national leaders had predicted that it would take five hundred years to settle the vast American West. However, in little more than the five decades between 1840 and 1890 much of the American wilderness had been surveyed, fenced, and crisscrossed with rail lines and telegraph wires. During this period, many formerly primitive villages had grown into burgeoning frontier towns.

These frontier towns were essentially blank canvases to which the trappings of "civilization" were to be applied, and women took important roles building these communities. They oversaw construction of schools and acted as teachers. They were instrumental in founding churches and opening libraries. They made paintings that preserved images of a rapidly disappearing wilderness. In some places, women fought for equal rights and the right to vote. And they were also moral champions who attempted to ban drinking, gambling, prostitution, crime, and violence.

Teachers

Nineteenth-century women were considered to be the arbiters of culture and civilization, and their roles in education were therefore, held in high esteem. Typical of this phenomenon was Grand Junction, Colorado, in the early 1880s. At that time, the town's first schoolteacher, Nannie Blain, was so revered that all the businesses within the town shut their doors at 2 P.M. so that everyone could gather to hear Miss Blain read and discuss the Bible.

The demand for teachers on the frontier was so great that an eastern organization, the National Board of Popular Education, took on the role of sponsoring teachers to move to the frontier. Close to one thousand single women teachers were part of the program in the decades following the founding of the program in 1846.

By working as teachers, single women were able to travel and live alone on the frontier while still retaining the respectability demanded of women in the nineteenth century. The stereotypical image of the upright and decent teacher popular at that time is described by Polly Welts Kaufman in *Women Teachers on the Frontier:* "The schoolmistress is the ideal woman about whom myths were made: moral, self-sacrificing, discreet, dedicated to the welfare of the children, and capable of bringing out the best in men. She is unconcerned with personal goals or needs."[87]

There are elements of truth to this stereotype because teaching on the frontier was a difficult task with few financial rewards. Teachers often taught up to forty students of all ages in one-room cabins. Martha Rodgers taught in a log cabin in Missouri in which the roof leaked so badly "that when it rains we take the books up & stand in one place till [the rain] begins to drop down & then we move to an other spot & then an other."[88] To add to Rodgers's problems, there was little heat in the leaky log cabin. To solve this, she saved her own money to buy a woodstove from a mail-order catalog. One Oklahoma teacher, Mabel Sharpe Beavers, went one step further, buying rough lumber and organizing her students to build a school with their own hands.

Teachers had to improvise in other ways too. Some had to make their own blackboards from slate or other materials.

Women who migrated to the frontier as teachers worked under very difficult conditions. They typically taught in crudely constructed cabins using very limited resources.

Seats and desks were constructed from boards laid upon logs or rocks. One teacher even borrowed the bones of skeletons from local doctors in order to teach her students the basics of human anatomy. Another brought her violin to school and played it to demonstrate basic musical skills.

Some women became public schoolteachers in order to educate their own children. These women, however, were also expected to continue performing the duties of a housewife. In 1887 Mary White of Nebraska wrote that she often taught from "a book [propped] in front of the wash-tub while I rubbed soiled clothes on the wash-board with both hands."[89]

Teachers who were not married faced great economic hardships. Although an annual salary of $150 plus room and board was the standard minimum wage for teachers at that time, many received much less. Arozina Perkins, who taught in Fort Des Moines, Iowa, in the 1850s, had so little money she could not afford clothes, as she wrote in her diary, "[I] expect when I get what clothes worn out that I [brought] with me I shall be obliged to wear a *blanket*, for . . . I never can make enough to clothe me decently."[90]

When town leaders—most often men—were reluctant to pay for schools, women contributed in various ways. In Oklahoma, the Ladies Aid Society raised money to pay teachers by organizing bazaars, dances, theatrical events, and other fundraisers.

Using creativity and skill, teachers succeeded remarkably well in some areas. For example, between 1870 and 1900, Kansas and Nebraska had some of the highest literacy rates in the country, higher than some states in the East.

Entering the Political Arena

Teachers sometimes went beyond educating children and used their skills in attempts to change society. For example, in the late 1850s, the Iowa State Teachers Association passed a resolution calling for woman suffrage—that is, woman's voting rights. In the 1860s the Iowa Assembly debated woman suffrage as a result of a petition signed by twenty-six women, many of them teachers. By the 1870s women from many backgrounds were organizing in frontier towns to discuss woman's rights. On occasion this was done through organizations such as the Grange, an association of both women and men farmers founded in 1867, as Glenda Riley writes in *The Female Frontier:*

> Literally thousands of prairie women contributed their time and energy to the woman-suffrage movement. . . . By the 1870s the Patrons of Hus-

> bandry, or Grange, units that were spreading over the prairie encouraged even more women to move from social to political action. Drawing women in on an equal basis with male members . . . the Grange provided a forum . . . for wider questions that directly affected farm women. Prairie Granges educated women in domestic skills, farm concerns, and women's issues. They also taught women how to lobby and think. . . . By the latter decades of the nineteenth century, female Grange members saw equal suffrage as their right. As one phrased it, "We demand equal suffrage without regard to sex or condition, so that the intelligent women of America may have the power to protect themselves, their homes, and their families."[91]

In general, woman suffrage was strongly opposed by most men. Not until 1920 would the U.S. Constitution be amended to make woman suffrage the law nationwide. However, by the late nineteenth century, four states—Colorado, Idaho, Wyoming, and Utah—had granted suffrage as a result of women demanding equal rights. Where women could vote, they also gained election to political office. In 1870, in South Pass City, Wyoming, Esther Morris became the nation's first female justice of the peace. The same year, Wyoming became the first place where women were allowed to serve on juries.

In 1887 women in Kansas were granted "municipal suffrage," allowing them to run for office and vote in local elections. After this law was passed, Meorda Salter, of Argonia, became the first woman in the United States to serve as a mayor. The next year in Oskaloosa, voters not only elected a female mayor but also elected women to fill all five seats on the city council.

While women made a few gains, the political theater was considered an unsuitable place for a lady, as Luna Kellie wrote: "I had been taught it was unwomanly to concern oneself with politics and that only the worst class of women would ever vote if they had a chance to."[92] Despite this conditioning, women became involved in politics when they believed that change could improve their communities.

Women as Reformers

If men opposed giving women the vote, they were equally reluctant to support another cause backed by many women: temperance, or the outlawing of alcoholic beverages. Driving the temperance movement was the fact that drinking was extremely common in frontier society.

Serving on the School Board

In the early 1900s western women made up a majority of teachers but rarely served on school boards. In Texas, however, Nellie M. Perry became the first woman board member of the Perryton Independent School District. She wryly recounts her call to duty in *Woman of the Plains:*

> The trustees of Perryton Independent School District have been from the beginning a very interesting group—six men and one woman for the first four years—I being the lone lorn woman.
>
> I was, like the other members, elected without any effort on my own part, and was surprised, pleasantly . . . when notified of my election. . . . On the day for the first meeting of the board, I had not been notified but had had an unofficial whisper in my ear with regard to the matter. . . . I was soon rushing to the scene of my future labors in behalf of the youth of the new town of Perryton, Texas.
>
> As I puffed into the Court House hall and looked anxiously about for my companions, I heard a medley of voices, following the sound of which I found myself in a room full of men in various stages of relaxation and hilarity. My appearance in the doorway was the signal for a sudden silence and a general paralytic stroke. . . . Somebody finally invited me in . . . but it was quite evident that I was unexpected. I was however duly "sworn" to many grand and noble objectives in life and the Perryton Independent School District—including a hectic declaration as to my Past that I had never fought a duel! . . . [We] were soon duly organized for work, a pitifully amateurish bunch to have charge of the education of youth.

Many men consumed liquor with breakfast, lunch, and dinner, and some continued drinking well into the night. Women were often the victims of this excess. Glenda Riley explains why temperance became an important issue to some women:

Told repeatedly that it was their duty to protect the home, plainswomen quickly moved into combat against alcohol as being one of the biggest threats to home and family. Some learned from firsthand experience about the destruction that liquor

> could wreak within their families. A young wife in Topeka during the 1890s endured her husband's ill temper, verbal abuse, loss of work time, expensive "cures" in Chicago, and finally his death as a result of alcohol.[93]

One of the first frontier women to preach temperance was Sarah Pellet, who moved to the boomtown of San Francisco in 1855. Although few miners wanted to hear about the evils of alcohol, Pellet cleverly attracted men to her lectures by dressing in what was called a bloomer costume. This outfit—a short skirt worn over loose trousers gathered at the ankles—drew men from all over town. As Franklin A. Buck describes the scene in *A Yankee Trader in the Gold Rush:* "When [Pellet] took to her stand on a dry goods box and commenced talking everyone ran [to her]. The saloons and stores were deserted. No dog fight ever drew together such a crowd. . . . Great country for women, isn't it?"[94]

While men might have been eager to see Pellet, they were less enthusiastic about her message. She promised her audience that if they would outlaw liquor, she would return to her native Boston and bring three thousand single women back to California. Pellet's temperance ideas did not find support, however, and one attendee, speaking for the crowd, wrote, "We thanked our lucky stars we were not tied to her for life."[95]

The idea of outlawing liquor spread quickly in the years following Pellet's solitary effort as groups of women began to organize temperance crusades. In Portland the Women's Temperance Prayer League (WTPL) was formed, and more than one thousand people signed the group's petition to forgo alcohol. Moved by this groundswell of support women began to invade saloons to sing hymns and recite Bible verses to the startled patrons. Although they were often met with verbal abuse—and showers of beer thrown by angry drunks—the temperance women returned to the saloons every day, and the harassment drove away customers, forcing several establishments to close.

Saloon Busters

The tactics of the WTPL were soon adapted by the Women's Christian Temperance Union (WCTU). Founded in 1874, the WCTU attracted large numbers of women from frontier towns west of the Mississippi. The organization provided a reason for many housewives to leave their kitchens and become politically involved for the first time. By 1890, with nearly 150,000 members across the country, the WCTU was, at that time, the largest women's organization in the history of the United States.

The WCTU was particularly active in Kansas, home to one of its most famous members, Carry Nation. After a brief marriage to a hopeless alcoholic in the late 1800s, Nation took on the role of "saloon buster" in the late 1890s. Technically Kansas was a "dry" state; it was illegal to make or sell alcohol. The state's drinkers skirted the law by imbibing in private clubs or special rooms set up behind drug stores, where liquor was sold ostensibly for "medicinal purposes." In an effort to put an end to this practice, Nation began marching into the makeshift bars in Medicine Lodge, Kansas to sing temperance songs to the men she described as "rum-soaked, whiskey-swelled, saturn-faced rummies."[96]

When this technique drove drinkers to Kiowa, twenty miles away, Nation took on the role of violent protester. She drove her buggy to Kiowa, armed with bricks, bottles, and rocks. In her autobiography, *The Use and Need of the Life of Carry A. Nation*, she describes what happened next:

Members of the Women's Christian Temperance Union march in Washington, D.C., on their way to the White House to present a petition supporting prohibition to the president.

> I began to throw [the rocks] at the mirror [inside the bar] and the bottles below the mirror. . . . From that I went to another saloon, until I had destroyed three, breaking some of the windows in the front of the building. In the last place . . . I threw a brick at the mirror, which was a very heavy one, and it did not break, but the brick fell and broke everything in its way. I began to look around for something that would break it. I was standing by a billiard table on which there was one ball. I said: "Thank God," and picked it up, threw it, and it made a hole in the mirror. . . . The other dive keepers closed up, stood in front of their places and would not let me come in. By this time, the streets were crowded with people; most of them seemed to look puzzled. . . . I stood in the middle of the street and spoke in this way: "I have destroyed three of your places of business, and if I have broken a statute of Kansas, put me in jail; if I am not a law-breaker your mayor and councilmen are. You must arrest one of us, for if I am not a criminal, they are."[97]

Within weeks, Nation was a national figure whose publicity in the press inspired similar acts throughout the United States. The publicity also helped to rapidly increase membership in the WCTU. Nation told reporters that she was on a religious mission, describing herself as "a bulldog running along at the feet of Jesus, barking at what he doesn't like."[98]

Women Editors

While Carry Nation busted up saloons, other WCTU members took a more genteel approach, utilizing the power of the written word to advance their cause. For example, Mary Frank Browne, who was president of the California WCTU, produced a monthly magazine called the *Pharos* in the 1880s and 1890s that served as a mouthpiece for the temperance movement. A typical issue had about twelve pages of essays, news, editorials, book reviews, and advertisements. Browne wrote articles and editorials and compiled news reports for the *Pharos*, which had a circulation of four thousand—quite a large press run for that time.

Browne was among an estimated 270 female magazine and newspaper editors working in the American West between 1854 and 1900. These women ranged in age from the thirteen-year-old Katherine Bragg who published the Tombstone, Arizona, *Bug Hunter* in 1891 to the eighty-year-old Mary Hayes-Chenoweth who edited the church magazine, the *True Life*, in San Jose, California.

Women who ran periodicals took on many nontraditional roles. They worked as advertising salespersons, typesetters, printers, paper cutters, and even delivery workers who dropped off the papers at central distribution points. More often women were reporters who wrote news articles, stories, and editorial and advice columns.

Writing for a Cause

Women who wrote for frontier newspapers and magazines often used their publications to broadcast their political views to local audiences. Some female authors, however, combined their writing talents with their social awareness to make an impact on the national dialogue. For example, Helen Hunt Jackson, one of the most renowned authors of the day, took Congress and the president of the United States to task over the treatment of Native Americans.

Jackson first gained national attention in the 1870s, writing articles about her travels on the American frontier for the *New York Times.* She was a well-respected author by 1879 when she heard a lecture by a Ponca Indian chief named Standing Bear who described the forcible removal of his people from their Nebraska reservation by the U.S. government.

Angered by what she heard, Jackson took on the role of zealous defender of Indian rights, circulating petitions, raising money, and writing letters to national publications. Jackson also poured her energies into the written word, writing a book called *Century of Dishonor*, which condemned the government's policies toward Native Americans, detailing the long history of broken treaties. When the book was published in 1881, Jackson sent a copy to every member of Congress, writing upon the covers: "Look upon your hands: They are stained with the blood of your relations."[99]

This scathing attack led President Chester Arthur to designate Jackson a special commissioner of Indian affairs in 1882. Jackson was the first woman to hold that position, and her work led her to travel to the California frontier towns such as San Diego and Los Angeles to investigate the condition of the so-called Mission Indians living nearby. Jackson wrote an eloquent report that called for the government to redress many of the Indians' grievances, but it was ignored. Frustrated, she set out to write a fictional work that would do for Native Americans what another popular work by a female author, *Uncle Tom's Cabin*, had done to turn people against slavery.

In 1884 Jackson wrote the novel *Ramona*, described by Ron Lackmann as a "sad tale about a half-breed Indian girl's doomed love affair with an Indian

Helen Hunt Jackson wrote books and articles condemning the government's treatment of Native Americans. Her work led to an appointment as commissioner of Indian affairs in Southern California.

youth and their mistreatment by whites."[100] Jackson's book became a best seller and was called "The Uncle Tom's Cabin of California." In 1887 it was said to inspire Congress to pass the Dawes Act, which granted every Native American 160 acres of land.

Portraying Life on Canvas

While Jackson described Indian life on the page, other women took on the role of artists, using paint, canvas, and sculpture to portray Native Americans, cowboys, miners, and the beauty of nature. These women faced hardships similar to earlier pioneers. They climbed mountains, endured snowstorms, and traveled into dangerous territory to record the world around them for future generations. One such artist was Helen Tanner Brodt, who became the first white woman to make the arduous climb up Mount Lassen near Redding, California, in 1864. She took on the role of mountain climber in order to paint the remarkable landscapes of the Sierra Nevada.

Brodt spent more than four decades recording California's missions, ranches, landscapes, and pioneers. She numbered among many female artists who had arrived in San Francisco during the gold rush era. By the late 1850s, San Francisco was the center for women artists in the West, and art exhibits were some of the most popular public attractions. When the San Francisco Mechanics' Institute sponsored an art fair in 1858, thousands of people attended. Among the works on display were paintings by fifty women.

As San Francisco grew into the cultural capital of the West Coast, several art schools opened that were popular with women. In 1873 there were forty-six women among the first sixty students at the California School of Design. Grace Carpenter Hudson was one of those students and later became known for her intimate portraits of local Pomo Indian children. These paintings came to represent an important record of a vanishing culture.

By 1885 there were so many women artists in San Francisco that the First Annual Exhibition of the Lady Artists featured more than 270 works by eighty-one female painters and sculptors. This exhibition, organized by women, was the first in the West to focus attention on female artists and showed that many had talents beyond what those amateurs referred to as "Sunday painters" possessed.

By 1890 there were an estimated eleven hundred female artists painting in the West. Although their work was sometimes dismissed by male art critics at the time, today, the work of western women artists is praised for its sensitivity and skillful execution. Like other women who lived and worked in growing cities on the frontier, their dedication earned them the respect in fields that they made uniquely their own.

Notes

Introduction: The American Frontier

1. Quoted in Barbara Welter, *Dimity Convictions: The American Woman in the Nineteenth Century.* Athens: Ohio University Press, 1976, p. 30.

Chapter 1: Women on the Appalachian Frontier

2. George Morgan Chinn, *Kentucky Settlements and Statehood, 1750–1800.* Frankfort: Kentucky Historical Society, 1975, p. 102.
3. George Washington Ranck, *Boonesborough.* Louisville, KY: J.P. Morton, 1901, p. 37.
4. Ranck, *Boonesborough*, p. 77.
5. Elizabeth F. Ellet, *The Pioneer Women of the West.* Philadelphia: Porter & Coates, 1873, p. 66.
6. Ellet, *The Pioneer Women of the West*, p. 93.
7. Quoted in Cathy Luchetti, *Home on the Range.* New York: Villard Books, 1993, p. 119.
8. Quoted in Luchetti, *Home on the Range*, p. 119.
9. Quoted in R. Carlyle Buley, *The Old Northwest: Pioneer Period, 1815–1840.* Bloomington: Indiana University Press, 1962, pp. 206–207.
10. Buley, *The Old Northwest*, p. 211.
11. Christina A. Aubin, "Quilt History," Quiltersbee.com, www.quiltersbee.com/qbqhisto.htm#Quilt_Bees.
12. Ellet, *The Pioneer Women of the West.* pp. 139–40.
13. Luchetti, *Home on the Range*, p. 116.

Chapter 2: Army Wives and Camp Followers

14. Quoted in Anne Bruner Eales, *Army Wives on the American Frontier.* Boulder, CO: Johnson Books, 1996, p. 118.
15. Glenda Riley, *The Female Frontier.* Lawrence: University of Kansas Press, 1988, p. 93.
16. Quoted in Luchetti, *Home on the Range*, p. 35.
17. Eales, *Army Wives on the American Frontier*, p. 11.
18. Eales, *Army Wives on the American Frontier*, pp. 65–66.
19. Quoted in Dana H. Prater, "Sabers and Soapsuds: Dragoon Women on the Frontier, 1833–1861," Kansas History

Gateway, September 17, 1992. www.ku.edu/history/ftp/articles/dragoon_women.txt.
20. Eales, *Army Wives on the American Frontier*, pp. 22–23.
21. Margaret Carrington, *Ab-sa-ra-ka, Home of the Crows: Being the Experience of an Officer's Wife on the Plains.* Philadelphia: J.B. Lippincott, 1868, p. 180.
22. Quoted in Carrington, *Ab-sa-ra-ka, Home of the Crows*, p. 153.
23. Quoted in Dee Brown, *The Gentle Tamers: Women of the Old Wild West.* Lincoln: University of Nebraska Press, 1995, p. 54.
24. Quoted in Darlis A. Miller, ed., *Above a Common Soldier.* Albuquerque: University of New Mexico Press, 1997, pp. 110–11.
25. Quoted in Prater, "Sabers and Soapsuds."
26. Sandra L. Myers, "Romance and Reality on the American Frontier: View of Army Wives," *Western Historical Quarterly* 14, no. 4, October 1983, p. 426.

Chapter 3: Women on the Trail

27. Quoted in Ann Kolodny, *The Land Before Her.* Chapel Hill: University of North Carolina Press, 1984.
28. Quoted in Lillian Schlissel, *Women's Diaries of the Westward Journey.* New York: Schocken Books, 1992, p. 148.
29. Quoted in Kolodny, *The Land Before Her*, p. 236.
30. Quoted in Schlissel, *Women's Diaries of the Westward Journey*, p. 28.
31. Quoted in Susan G. Butruille, *Women's Voices from the Oregon Trail.* Boise, ID: Tamarack Books, 1993, p. 97.
32. Butruille, *Women's Voices from the Oregon Trail*, pp. 6–7.
33. Quoted in Butruille, *Women's Voices from the Oregon Trail*, p. 55.
34. Quoted in Kenneth L. Holmes, *Covered Wagon Women*, vol. 1. Lincoln: University of Nebraska Press, 1983, p. 217.
35. Quoted in Schlissel, *Women's Diaries of the Westward Journey*, p. 179.
36. Quoted in Schlissel, *Women's Diaries of the Westward Journey*, p. 36.
37. Eliza G. Farnham, *California, Indoors and Out; or, How We Farm, Mine, and Live Generally in the Golden State.* New York: Dix, Edwards, 1856, pp. 298–99.
38. Quoted in Judith E. Greenberg and Helen Carey McKeever, *A Pioneer Woman's Memoir.* New York: Franklin Watts, 1995, pp. 34–35.
39. Quoted in Greenberg and McK-

eever, *A Pioneer Woman's Memoir*, p. 87

40. Quoted in Schlissel, *Women's Diaries of the Westward Journey*, p. 180.
41. Quoted in Brown, *The Gentle Tamers*, p. 37.
42. Quoted in Schlissel, *Women's Diaries of the Westward Journey*, p. 168.
43. Quoted in Schlissel, *Women's Diaries of the Westward Journey*, p. 60.
44. Quoted in Schlissel, *Women's Diaries of the Westward Journey*, p. 41.
45. Schlissel, *Women's Diaries of the Westward Journey*, p. 14.
46. Quoted in Butruille, *Women's Voices from the Oregon Trail*, p. 25.
47. Quoted in Kolodny, *The Land Before Her*, p. 239.
48. Quoted in Kolodny, *The Land Before Her*, p. 240.

Chapter 4: Native American Women

49. Theda Perdue, ed., *Sifters: Native American Women's Lives.* New York: Oxford University Press, 2001, p. 5.
50. Carolyn Niethammer, *Daughters of the Earth*. New York: Collier Books, 1977, p. xii.
51. Niethammer, *Daughters of the Earth*, p. 145.
52. Glenda Riley, *Women and Indians on the Frontier, 1825–1915*. Albuquerque: University of New Mexico Press, 1984, p. 171.
53. Quoted in Riley, *Women and Indians on the Frontier, 1825–1915*, p. 173–74.
54. Niethammer, *Daughters of the Earth*, p. 165.
55. Quoted in Niethammer, *Daughters of the Earth*, p. 174.
56. Quoted in Perdue, *Sifters,* p. 101.
57. Quoted in Perdue, *Sifters,* p. 106.
58. Quoted in R.B. Stratton, *Life Among the Indians; or, the Captivity of the Oatman Girls Among the Apache and Mohave Indians.* San Francisco: Grabhorn Press, 1935, p. 157.

Chapter 5: Women in Mining Camps and Towns

59. Quoted in Christiane Fischer, ed., *Let Them Speak for Themselves: Women in the American West, 1849–1900.* New York: E.P. Dutton, 1977, p. 52.
60. Quoted in Jo Ann Levy, *They Saw the Elephant: Women in the California Gold Rush.* Norman: University of Oklahoma Press, 1992, p. 91.
61. Quoted in Levy, *They Saw the Elephant*, p. 93.

62. Quoted in Levy, *They Saw the Elephant*, p. 94.
63. Quoted in Luchetti, *Home on the Range*, p. 66.
64. Quoted in Luchetti, *Home on the Range*, p. 66.
65. Quoted in Levy, *They Saw the Elephant*, p. 102.
66. Quoted in Fischer, *Let Them Speak for Themselves*, pp. 43, 45.
67. Quoted in Levy, *They Saw the Elephant*, p. 98.
68. Quoted in Levy, *They Saw the Elephant*, p. 110.
69. Quoted in Ronald Dean Miller, *Shady Ladies of the West*. Tucson: Westernlore Press, 1985, p. 77.
70. Cathy Luchetti and Carol Olwell, *Women of the West*, Berkeley, CA: Antelope Island Press, 1982, pp. 31, 33.

Chapter 6: Ranchers and Cowgirls

71. Elizabeth Clair Flood, *Cowgirls: Women of the Wild West*. Santa Fe, NM: Zon International, 2000, p. 15.
72. Quoted in William H. Forbis, *The Cowboys*. Alexandria, VA: Time-Life Books, 1973, p. 71.
73. Quoted in Candace Savage, *Cowgirls*. Vancouver, BC: Greystone Books, 1996, p. 5.
74. Quoted in Jo Ella Powell Exley, ed., *Texas Tears and Texas Sunshine*. College Station: Texas A&M University, 1985, pp. 218–19.
75. Savage, *Cowgirls*, pp. 4–5.
76. Quoted in Exley, *Texas Tears and Texas Sunshine*, p. 235.
77. Quoted in Savage, *Cowgirls*, p. 9.
78. Quoted in Flood, *Cowgirls*, p. 16.
79. Quoted in Savage, *Cowgirls*, p. 8.
80. Quoted in Flood, *Cowgirls*, p. 17.
81. Joyce Gibson Roach, *The Cowgirls*. Houston: Cordovan, 1978, p. 41.
82. Quoted in Roach, *The Cowgirls*, p. 42.
83. Roach, *The Cowgirls*, p. 76.
84. Roach, *The Cowgirls*, pp. 75–76.
85. Quoted in Pan Historia, "Home of Jo Monaghan," 2003. www.panhistoria.com/Stacks/Novels/Character_Homes/home.php?CharID=6080.
86. Quoted in Flood, *Cowgirls*, p. 62.

Chapter 7: Women in Frontier Towns

87. Polly Welts Kaufman, *Women Teachers on the Frontier*. New Haven, CT: Yale University Press, 1984, p. vxii.
88. Quoted in Kaufman, *Women Teachers on the Frontier*, p. 183.
89. Quoted in Joan Swallow Reiter, *The Women*. Alexandria, VA: Time-Life Books, 1978, p. 90.
90. Quoted in Kaufman, *Women*

Teachers on the Frontier, p. 138.

91. Riley, *The Female Frontier*, p. 168.
92. Quoted in Riley, *The Female Frontier*, p. 187.
93. Riley, *The Female Frontier*, p. 178.
94. Franklin A. Buck, *A Yankee Trader in the Gold Rush*. Boston: Houghton Mifflin, 1930, p. 149.
95. Quoted in Jeanne Hamilton Watson, ed., *To the Land of Gold and Wickedness: The 1848–59 Diary of Lorena L. Hays*. St. Louis, MO: Patrice Press, 1988, p. 215.
96. Carry Nation, *The Use and Need of the Life of Carry A. Nation*. Topeka, KS: F.M. Steves & Sons, 1905, p. 94.
97. Nation, *The Use and Need of the Life of Carry A. Nation*, pp. 71–72.
98. Quoted in Women's History, "Carry Nation," 1999. http://womenshistory.about.com/gi/dynamic/offsite.htm?site=http%3A%2F%2Fwww.pbs.org%2Fwgbh%2Famex%2F1900%2Fpeo-pleevents% 2Fpande4.html.
99. Quoted in The Glass Ceiling, "Helen Hunt Jackson," 2000. www.theglassceiling.com/biographies/bio16.htm.
100. Ron Lackmann, *Women of the Western Frontier in Fact, Fiction and Film*. Jefferson, NC: McFarland, 1997, p. 120.

For Further Reading

Paula Bartley and Cathy Loxton, *Plains Women: Women of the American West.* New York: Cambridge University Press, 1991. Part of the Women in History series, this book explores the way the social lives of frontier women were affected by their environment.

Liza Ketchum, *Into a New Country: Eight Remarkable Women of the West.* Boston: Little, Brown, 2000. Biographies of western women who rode the Santa Fe Trail, worked as performers at gold camps, rallied support for Indians, and others.

Cathy Luchetti and Carol Olwell, *Women of the West.* Berkeley, CA: Antelope Island Press, 1982. Hundreds of original photos from the frontier days fill out this book of extensive firsthand accounts of western life taken from women's diaries, letters, and books.

Mary Barmeyer O'Brien, *Heart of the Trail: The Stories of Eight Wagon Train Women.* Helena, MT: Falcon, 1997. The triumphs and tribulations of eight women who crossed the American frontier by wagon based on letters and diaries written at the time.

Candace Savage, *Cowgirls.* Vancouver, BC: Greystone Books, 1996. The stories of real-life cattle queens, bronco riders, lady bandits, and ranch women, with hundreds of old photographs, posters, and paintings of cowgirls.

Harriet Sigerman, *Land of Many Hands: Women in the American West.* New York: Oxford University Press, 1997. The fascinating stories of women on the burgeoning western frontier between 1840 and 1900.

Works Consulted

Books

Sherilyn Cox Bennion, *Equal to the Occasion: Women Editors of the Nineteenth-Century West.* Reno: University of Nevada Press, 1990. An interesting study of frontier women who edited newspapers and magazines, using the written word to give voice to community concerns during a lawless era.

Virginia Marie Bouvier, *Women and the Conquest of California, 1542–1840.* Tucson: University of Arizona Press, 2001. The roles women played during the European and American settlement of California.

Dee Brown, *The Gentle Tamers: Women of the Old Wild West.* Lincoln: University of Nebraska Press, 1995. First published in 1958, this exploration of the western frontier describes the hope, tragedy, humor, and boredom that governed women's lives between 1850 and 1880.

Franklin A. Buck, *A Yankee Trader in the Gold Rush.* Boston: Houghton Mifflin, 1930. A compilation of letters written by a successful trader as he traveled through San Francisco and the gold country in the early 1850s.

R. Carlyle Buley, *The Old Northwest: Pioneer Period, 1815–1840.* Bloomington: Indiana University Press, 1962. The history, culture, and industry of present-day Ohio, Indiana, Illinois, and Michigan.

Mary Bunton, *A Bride on the Old Chisholm Trail in 1886.* San Antonio, TX: Naylor, 1939. Tales of life on the cow trail written by a society "belle" who left the East to become a Texas cowgirl after marrying into a powerful pioneer family.

Susan G. Butruille, *Women's Voices from the Oregon Trail.* Boise, ID: Tamarack Books, 1993. A narrative of life along the two-thousand-mile Oregon Trail during the 1840s in the words of women's songs, poetry, diaries, and recipes.

Calamity Jane, *Life and Adventures of Calamity Jane.* Fairfield, WA: Ye Galleon Press, 1969. The short autobiography of the famed woman who was a Pony Express rider and an army scout in the nineteenth century.

Margaret Carrington, *Ab-sa-ra-ka, Home of the Crows: Being the Experience of an Officer's Wife on the Plains.*

Philadelphia: J.B. Lippincott, 1868. The memoirs of the wife of the commander at Fort Kearny in present-day Nebraska during the height of hostilities between the U.S. Army and the Native Americans of the plains.

Andrew R.L. Cayton and Fredrika J. Teute, eds., *Contact Points: American Frontiers from the Mohawk Valley to the Mississippi, 1750–1830.* Chapel Hill: University of North Carolina Press, 1998. Eleven essays that examine the interaction of Indians and European and African settlers on the frontier that lay on the eastern half of North America.

George Morgan Chinn, *Kentucky Settlements and Statehood, 1750–1800.* Frankfort: Kentucky Historical Society, 1975. A thorough history of Kentucky's early years and the role settlers played in the trans-Appalachian West.

Harry S. Drago, *Notorious Ladies of the Frontier.* New York: Dodd, Mead, 1969. The activities and accomplishments of various dance-hall girls, prostitutes, female outlaws, and other colorful women of the West.

Anne Bruner Eales, *Army Wives on the American Frontier.* Boulder, CO: Johnson Books, 1996. A well-written, carefully researched, and comprehensive look at the lives and roles of women who traveled the West with their husbands, who served in the U.S. Army.

Elizabeth F. Ellet, *The Pioneer Women of the West.* Philadelphia: Porter & Coates, 1873. First published in 1852, this book is among the first to document the roles of women on the American frontier, from the wilds of western North Carolina to the old Northwest Territory of Ohio, Michigan, and elsewhere.

Jo Ella Powell Exley, ed., *Texas Tears and Texas Sunshine.* College Station: Texas A&M University, 1985. The frontier years in Texas through the eyes of women authors who wrote extensively about their many interesting experiences in the early years of the Lone Star State.

Eliza G. Farnham, *California, In-doors and Out; or, How We Farm, Mine, and Live Generally in the Golden State.* New York: Dix, Edwards, 1856. A book written during the gold rush era meant as a guide to those who planned to immigrate to California.

Christiane Fischer, ed., *Let Them Speak for Themselves: Women in the American West, 1849–1900.* New York: E.P. Dutton, 1977. The letters, diaries, and reminiscences of twenty-five women pioneers in California, Nevada, and Arizona.

Elizabeth Clair Flood, *Cowgirls: Women of the Wild West.* Santa Fe, NM: Zon International, 2000. A big, colorful book with text describing the lives of cowgirls, along with photos, drawings, posters, and pictures of clothing that give life to the cowgirl legend.

William H. Forbis, *The Cowboys.* Alexandria, VA: Time-Life Books, 1973. A fun, interesting book about the real lives of cowboys and cowgirls.

Judith E. Greenberg and Helen Carey McKeever, *A Pioneer Woman's Memoir.* New York: Franklin Watts, 1995. The memoir of Arabella Clemens Fulton, a young woman from Missouri who caught "Oregon Fever" in 1864 and headed to the West Coast on the Oregon Trail.

Joan R. Gundersen, *To Be Useful to the World.* New York: Twayne, 1996. A detailed and well-researched account of the lives of colonial women between 1740 and 1790.

Kenneth L. Holmes, *Covered Wagon Women.* Vol. 1. Lincoln: University of Nebraska Press, 1983. Letters and diaries from the Oregon Trail during the years between 1840 and 1849, reproduced in their original quirky jargon that brings alive the speech of the day.

Julie Roy Jeffrey, *Frontier Women.* New York: Hill and Wang, 1979. A historic examination of the western frontier in the second half of the nineteenth century based on diaries and letters written by female pioneers.

Polly Welts Kaufman, *Women Teachers on the Frontier.* New Haven, CT: Yale University Press, 1984. Firsthand accounts of women who traveled the frontier before the Civil War, working as teachers under the most primitive conditions.

Ann Kolodny, *The Land Before Her.* Chapel Hill: University of North Carolina Press, 1984. The view of the frontier was sold to women as a land of milk and honey. The reality of the hardships is recorded here in diaries and letters.

Ron Lackmann, *Women of the Western Frontier in Fact, Fiction and Film.* Jefferson, NC: McFarland, 1997. An interesting comparison of glamorized women's roles in the Wild West as portrayed in movies contrasted with the often harsh reality of life for prostitutes, outlaws, cowgirls, traveling entertainers, and others.

Jo Ann Levy, *They Saw the Elephant: Women in the California Gold Rush.* Norman: University of Oklahoma Press, 1992. Women's lives on the adventure to the gold country, which was referred to as "seeing the elephant" for its exotic, mythical qualities.

Cathy Luchetti, *Home on the Range.* New York: Villard Books, 1993. A culinary history of the American West with descriptions of frontier food—and near starvation—taken largely from diaries and letters of women.

Wilma Mankiller and Michael Wallis, *Mankiller: A Chief and Her People.* New York: St. Martin's, 1993. This inspirational and insightful autobiography of Wilma Mankiller also recounts three hundred years of Native American history.

Darlis A. Miller, ed., *Above a Common Soldier.* Albuquerque: University of New Mexico Press, 1997. The adventures of Frank and Mary Clarke as they traveled the West with Frank serving as an officer in the U.S. Army, taken from letters to relatives and journal entries.

Ronald Dean Miller, *Shady Ladies of the West.* Tucson: Westernlore Press, 1985. The stories of female entertainers, prostitutes, gamblers, and murderers who populated the Wild West.

Carry Nation, *The Use and Need of the Life of Carry A. Nation.* Topeka, KS: F.M. Steves & Sons, 1905. The autobiography of the saloon-busting Christian temperance leader who was famous on the frontier in the early 1900s.

Carolyn Niethammer, *Daughters of the Earth.* New York: Collier Books, 1977. The lives and legends of Native American women from birth to death and the spiritual world beyond.

Theda Perdue, ed., *Sifters: Native American Women's Lives.* New York: Oxford University Press, 2001. Essays on Native American women's roles in American culture written by historians, anthropologists, and several Native American authors.

Nellie M. Perry, *Woman of the Plains.* Sandra Gail Teichmann, Ed. College Station: Texas A&M University Press, 2000. The journals and stories of Nellie Perry as she traveled to Texas, Montana, and elsewhere during the waning years of the nineteenth century and early years of the twentieth century.

George Washington Ranck, *Boonesborough.* Louisville, KY: J.P. Morton, 1901. The founding, pioneer struggles, Indian experiences, and Revolutionary War annals of one of Kentucky's original settlements.

Joan Swallow Reiter, *The Women.* Alexandria, VA: Time-Life Books, 1978. Part of The Old West series, this book explores the roles of women on the frontier and illustrates their lives with source documents, pictures, paintings, and maps.

Glenda Riley, *The Female Frontier.* Lawrence: University of Kansas Press, 1988. A scholarly work that looks at the employment, homes, and culture of women on the prairies and the plains.

———, *Women and Indians on the Fron-*

tier, 1825–1915. Albuquerque: University of New Mexico Press, 1984. A book that examines the relationships between white female settlers on the frontier and Native American women.

Joyce Gibson Roach, *The Cowgirls.* Houston: Cordovan, 1978. A colorful exploration of the roles played by horsewomen on western ranches and in rodeos, Wild West shows, pulp fiction, and movies.

Lillian Schlissel, *Women's Diaries of the Westward Journey.* New York: Schocken Books, 1992. Descriptions of life along the Oregon Trail and other trails, written between the 1840s and the 1860s by travelers heading west.

Laurence I. Seidman, *Fools of '49.* New York: Knopf, 1976. A book about the California gold rush based on journals, letters, and diaries of those who were there. Dozens of sad, funny, and informational quotes from miners and others.

Joanna L. Stratton, *Pioneer Women: Voices from the Kansas Frontier.* New York: Simon and Schuster, 1981. Daily life on the plains taken from hundreds of original manuscripts collected by the great-grandmother of the author, who discovered them in an attic in 1975.

R.B. Stratton, *Life Among the Indians; or, the Captivity of the Oatman Girls Among the Apache and Mohave Indians.* San Francisco: Grabhorn Press, 1935. The story of two young settler women who were kidnapped by the Apaches and later sold to the Mohaves.

Larry D. Underwood, *Dreams of Glory: Women of the Old West.* Lincoln, NE: Dageforde, 1997. The antics of restless women who moved to the West hoping to find riches, justice, or simply a better life.

Maurine Carr Ward, ed., *Winter Quarters: The 1846–1848 Life Writings of Mary Haskin Parker Richards.* Logan: Utah State University Press, 1999. The experiences of a young Mormon woman as she travels across the Iowa frontier on her way to Utah.

Jeanne Hamilton Watson, ed., *To the Land of Gold and Wickedness: The 1848–59 Diary of Lorena L. Hays.* St. Louis, MO: Patrice Press, 1988. A memorable diary of an educated pioneer woman who speaks of the joys and hardships of the overland trail and life during the gold rush.

Barbara Welter, *Dimity Convictions: The American Woman in the Nineteenth Century.* Athens: Ohio University Press, 1976. The lives of middle-class nineteenth-century American women, characterized by domesticity, piety, purity, and submissiveness.

Gene Weltfish, *The Lost Universe.* Lincoln: University of Nebraska Press, 1965. Beginning in 1928, the author studied myths, tales, and life experiences of elders to write about pre-reservation Pawnee life. Weltfish is an anthropologist fluent in the Pawnee language, and her book is one of the most complete ethnologies of the Pawnee ever written.

Periodical

Sandra L. Myers, "Romance and Reality on the American Frontier: View of Army Wives," *Western Historical Quarterly* 14, no. 4, October 1983. An article about the roles army wives assumed at military posts on the frontier.

Internet Sources

Christina A. Aubin, "Quilt History," Quiltersbee.com, www.quiltersbee.com/qbqhisto.htm#Quilt_Bees. A Web site dedicated to quilting, quilting bees, and quilting history.

The Glass Ceiling, "Helen Hunt Jackson," 2000. www.theglassceiling.com/biographies/bio16.htm. A biography of a gifted author who used her fame to fight for equal rights for Native Americans.

Pan Historia, "Home of Jo Monaghan," 2003. www.panhistoria.com/Stacks/Novels/Character_Homes/home.php?CharID=6080. A Web site dedicated to the cowgirl who spent her entire adult life dressed as a man, working a small ranch in Idaho.

Dana H. Prater, "Sabers and Soapsuds: Dragoon Women on the Frontier, 1833–1861," Kansas History Gateway, September 17, 1992. www.ku.edu/history/ftp/articles/dragoon_women.txt. An informative article about women's roles among the mounted battalion of soldiers known as the dragoons who fought Indians on the plains in the mid-1800s.

Women's History, "Carry Nation," 1999. http://womenshistory.about.com/gi/dynamic/offsite.htm?site=http%3A%2F%2Fwww.pbs.org%2Fwgbh%2Famex%2F1900%2Fpeopleevents%2Fpande4.html. A brief biography of the temperance leader from the companion site to the Public Broadcasting System's TV show "America 1900," part of the *American Experience* series.

Index

Picture Credits

Cover: © AKG-Images
© Bettmann/CORBIS, 44, 75, 85
© CORBIS, 26
Hulton/Archive by Getty Images, 67, 81, 90
Library of Congress, 14, 51, 82
© National Portrait Gallery, Smithsonian Institution/Art Resource, NY, 64
North Wind Picture Archives, 19, 44, 52, 93
Picture History, 31
Prints Old and Rare, 7
© Stapleton Collection/CORBIS, 56

About the Author

Stuart A. Kallen is the author of more than 170 nonfiction books for children and young adults. He has written on topics ranging from the theory of relativity to the history of rock and roll. In addition, Mr. Kallen has written award-winning children's videos and television scripts. In his spare time, Stuart A. Kallen is a singer/songwriter/guitarist in San Diego.